ADVANCE PRAISE FOR *RENEGADE MARKETING*

"Drew has written a provocative book that at once challenges and inspires B2B marketers to reinvent their roles and impact. Written in an artful, easy-to-read narrative style, Drew's book is a perfect reflection of who he is, challenging the status quo in a way that works. A must read for B2B marketers everywhere."

—Kimberly A. Whitler, Frank M. Sands senior associate professor of business administration, Darden School of Business, and author of *Positioning for Advantage*

"No one in the industry has gleaned more CMO insights than Drew. He has synthesized hundreds of conversations into a fun-to-read and immensely valuable B2B marketing playbook. I highly recommend it to anyone who wants to become a more effective marketer."

—Grant Johnson, CMO of Emburse

"In *Renegade Marketing*, Neisser nails one of the biggest obstacles hamstringing B2B brands—our marketing approach has become way too complex. Amen! I appreciate the way he both challenges and inspires CMOs to simplify, providing a blueprint with real-world examples on how to cut through the clutter, rethink our approach to customer engagement, and measure what matters."

—Scott Vaughan, B2B CMO and growth executive

"This book provides an in-depth look at B2B marketing with helpful takeaways in every chapter. I found the chapter on marketing technology particularly insightful, as it provided guidance for marketing practitioners on a very complex and confusing subject. What is the appropriate amount of technology? What works and what doesn't? Where to find it, and how to measure its results?"

—Martha Reeves, Ph.D, professor of the practice, director of markets and management studies at Duke University

"Drew has created the definitive guide for B2B marketers who want to crush their goals and build a better world. He masterfully packages key lessons from decades of experience, dozens of case studies, and hundreds of interviews with the best CMOs in the world. Buy this book today."

—Dan Marks, executive vice president and CMO

"With laser clarity, Drew Neisser lays out an engaging blueprint for success in B2B marketing, business growth, and career advancement. Soberingly practical!"

—Marshall Poindexter, CMO, OpenEye Scientific

"What's the best way to learn marketing? Talk to other marketers. And that's what Drew Neisser does so well. His book isn't just one guy's thoughts about marketing; it's a collection of practical insights and advice from some of the top marketers out there. Every chapter is chock-full of actionable marketing ideas that you can implement in your business today."

—Jeff Perkins, CEO (former CMO) of ParkMobile

"I really love how this invaluable guide to B2B marketing leads with courage as a foundational trait of successful CMOs. Without courage, marketers are merely caretakers of the status quo!"

—John F. Ellett, CEO of Springbox, author of *The CMO Manifesto*

"This remarkably inspiring B2B playbook is a must-read for marketers of any level. It lays out a powerful framework for enabling your B2B marketing strategies to really deliver results in a sea of fairly uninspiring, me-too approaches that unfortunately litter the landscape of B2B marketing."

—Kevin Sellers, CMO of Ping Identity

"This is the first B2B marketing book I've read that truly understands the critical role employees play in brand growth. If you buy this only to read Chapter 7: Engage Employees First, you will get more than your money's worth, given all the savvy guidance Drew provides."

—Ran Avrahamy, CMO of AppsFlyer

"I've been a CMO for six years and a GTM advisor to over twenty-five companies and still found many useful insights in Neisser's new book. This is a must-have resource for B2B marketers of any level."

—Meagen Eisenberg, CMO of TripActions

"Drew's fresh insights about B2B branding blow the dust off conventional wisdom. I've benefited immensely from his smarts and know you will too! I love this book."

—James Gardner, marketing strategist, educator, and speaker

"In a sea of marketing books, Drew Neisser's provides a life raft for B2B companies that so often get ignored. Drew's simple framework, inspiring case studies, fascinating interviews, and impressive professional experience all combine to create the go-to marketing handbook for B2Bs. Stop reading blurbs and go buy this book right now! Because if you don't, your competition will."

—Dan Gingiss, author of *The Experience Maker: How To Create Remarkable Experiences That Your Customers Can't Wait To Share*

"The very essence of being a renegade begins with having the courage to challenge the norm. *Renegade Marketing* delivers a powerful playbook for B2B marketing success, challenging CMOs to force change as a way of gaining brand recognition and achieving market dominance."

—Michael Welts, CMO of Wasabi

"In this important manuscript, Drew uncovers gold nuggets from many of the best and brightest CMOs, addressing the too-often ignored world of B2B marketing. Offering wise counsel to aspiring CMOs, this book will make you not just a better marketer but also a better leader."

—Greg Welch, partner and CMO practice leader of Spencer Stuart

"As cybersecurity and tech-focused CMO, I found Drew's 12-step guide to B2B marketing incredibly insightful and inspiring. Every marketer out there will find value in this high-impact book."

—Dan Lowden, CMO of Human Security

"I loved Neisser's first book, and his latest book all but guarantees you'll become an effective B2B marketer! If you are committed to growing your B2B marketing, this book is a must."

—Bill Carmody, bestselling author, TEDx storyteller, CMO and head of coaching for Positive Intelligence

"Business school curricula have largely ignored B2B marketing. If you're longing to learn, start with this book. It provides countless insights on how to gain a competitive advantage in a B2B environment. The book is breezy, easy to read, astute, and practical."

—Sam Craig, emeritus professor of marketing at NYU's Stern School of Business

"An amazing and practical guide focused specifically on B2B brands and the marketing strategies we need, this book by Drew Neisser makes the complex simple and is a must read for B2B marketers and executives who are looking to drive growth for their business."

—Michael Brenner, CEO of Marketing Insider Group and author of *Mean People Suck*

"Drew is an expert in B2B marketing, and this book is a great road map for how to build an amazing brand."

—John Hall, author of *Top of Mind* and chief strategist at Relevance.com.

"If I managed a B2B brand, I would make sure every person on my team read Drew Neisser's book *Renegade Marketing: 12 Steps to Building Unbeatable B2B Brands*. Drew utilizes his forty-plus years of marketing experience and over 450 interviews with CMOs to provide a 12-step playbook that will enable any and every B2B brand to up their game. Make *Renegade Marketing* required reading!"

—Brian Moran, founder and CEO of Small Business Edge

"Drew Neisser, the "Renegade Marketer," distinguishes himself as a valued leader in the tough world of B2B marketing. He's a renegade because he consistently dares to be bold, original, and honest. His book is a treasure chest of insightful and actionable strategies and techniques. Reading it is an investment in business success."

—*Glen Gilmore*, "man of action" (*TIME* magazine), author of *Social Media Law for Business*, and adjunct instructor of digital marketing at Rutgers University School of Business.

"With the publishing of *Renegade Marketing: 12 Steps to Building Unbeatable B2B Brands*, Drew Neisser delivers the ultimate guide on B2B Branding, from personal experience, trial and error, case histories, and down-to-earth smarts. Don't miss your chance to learn from the best."

—Ted Rubin, speaker, provocateur, and coauthor of *Return on Relationship*

"If the point of marketing is to stand out from the competition, why do so many marketers slavishly follow the herd? Drew Neisser's *Renegade Marketing* not only reminds you why it's vital to your business that you break from the pack but also shows you how, with pages of real-world strategies, insights, and tactics drawn from Drew's interviews with hundreds of CMOs—CMOs who, by daring to be different, have beaten their competition, driven sales, increased customer loyalty, and improved employee retention. So now you can too."

—Martin Bihl, executive creative director of LevLane and editor-in-chief of the-agency-review.com

"A truly fresh way to think about B2B branding. Don't miss Chapter 9, where Drew explains the exciting concept of "Sell Through Service"—brilliant. Packed with interesting stories, this is a great read."

—Ruth P. Stevens, president of eMarketing Strategy and author of *Maximizing Lead Generation: The Complete Guide for B2B Marketers*

"Focus drives results. Drew's framework ensures you're relentlessly focused and equipped to deliver amazing marketing!"

—Ed Rusch, CMO of Blueridge Global

"Great read—in fact, I reread many parts several times! I like how Drew ends each chapter with three key takeaways. His book is a good reminder of how a good purpose-driven statement can be a beacon for the holy grail: employee engagement, customer retention, and acquisition endeavors."

—Connie O'Brien, senior vice president of
marketing and digital operations

"Drew provides insightful, important information and actionable steps B2B marketers can take to differentiate their brands, drive demand, and cultivate customer champions. With real-world examples from leading marketing executives and top brands, you'll learn from some of the best and walk away feeling inspired and empowered to transform your organization's marketing machine."

—Julie Feller, head of marketing for U.S. Legal Support

"Drew Neisser's entertaining new book offers a treasure trove of marketing insights and inspiration for the often-ignored B2B marketer."

—Jed Alpert, B2B CMO

"Drew's 12-step B2B playbook is a refreshing mix of the strategic and the practical, all the while being brought to life by entertaining examples. I finished my read energized and with a list of items I wanted to get done with the help of Centric's marketing department."

—Mike Brannan, CMO of Centric Consulting

"I love a book that is full of wisdom and great stories and that is also easy to read. *Renegade Marketing* hits all these notes. Check this out if you want to learn how to become the savviest of B2B marketers and have fun while doing it."

—Michael Schein, author of *The Hype Handbook*

RENEGADE
MARKETING

12 Steps to Building
Unbeatable B2B Brands

RENEGADE
MARKETING

DREW NEISSER

Foreword by Brent Adamson

Published by CMO Huddles, New York City
http://cmohuddles.com

Edited and designed by Girl Friday Productions
www.girlfridayproductions.com

Cover design: Paul Barrett
Project management: Sara Addicott
Editorial: Tiffany Taing

ISBN (hardcover): 978-1-7372125-4-6
ISBN (paperback): 978-1-7372125-1-5
ISBN (ebook): 978-1-7372125-2-2

Library of Congress Control Number: 2021912153

To my ever-inspiring grown-up kids, Emma and Carl

CONTENTS

FOREWORD

No matter what you sell, how you sell, or where you sell, we all sell the same thing. We sell change.

Whether it's convincing a company to switch from one supplier to another, swap an old approach for a new one, or move from do-it-yourself to an outsourcing partner, we're all trying to get our customers to do something different. In fact, even with existing customers, we're invariably seeking to grow—which from a *customer's* perspective means switching from a status quo to a new kind of behavior. Bottom line, B2B suppliers aren't so much in the "solutions" business as they are in the "change" business.

Why does that matter? Because it's the one thing most organizations will seek to avoid whenever possible: change. It's hard. It's disruptive. It's expensive. It's risky. Or at least it's *perceived* to be. At the end of the day, this is why selling complex solutions often feels so hard. The very thing we sell is what customers most likely seek to avoid.

In a world like this, marketing really matters. And for marketers, the right mindset matters even more. Because if marketers' primary mission in driving growth is to actually lead customers to embrace change, then the kinds of questions marketers must ask look very different.

Traditionally, marketers broadly focus on two critical questions:

1. How do customers think about us (i.e., our brand, our product)?
2. How do customers compare us to others (i.e., competitors, alternate approaches)?

But notice: both of these questions are deeply supplier centric, specifically designed to change the way a customer thinks about a *supplier* rather than the way a customer thinks about their own organization or current course of action.

Instead, a far more productive question would be:

"How do customers think about *themselves*?"

Not just, "What are their fears or aspirations?" but far more concretely, "What are the specific organizational obstacles inside their organization making the pain of change seem so high?" After all, if we sell change, then we need to teach customers that the pain of "same" is far greater than the pain of change. And we can only do that if we've mapped in detail each side of that change dynamic, completely agnostic of any given supplier capability.

The world's best marketing isn't about changing customers' supplier perceptions, but rather changing customers' *self*-perceptions.

Or, as Drew puts it in this wonderfully engaging book, renegade marketers don't just think differently, they successfully inspire others to *act* differently. Marketing isn't a beauty contest (the best logo, the coolest colors, the snappiest tag line), it's about understanding human behavior at a sufficiently deep level to lead customers to appreciate, embrace, and then act on the kinds of change that can materially improve their own organization.

In fact, at its absolute, aspirational best, renegade marketing is about making the world a better place. And that is going to take courage, creativity, insight, and most importantly, a deep sense of humility and empathy.

For me, that's the critical red thread moving through Drew's CATS framework: empathy and humility. Renegade marketers don't just "cut through" the cluttered world of marketing messages to gain attention; they cut through the status quo to drive productive change—where "productive" is defined solely in terms of a customer's choosing. Renegade marketers see a world that customers would unquestionably perceive as better if only they were able to conceive of that possibility in the first place.

But that kind of imagination—that kind of "renegade thinking"— requires viewing the world through a completely different lens. To be sure, it starts from the customer's perspective, but then asks, "What else is there? What else could there be?" In that way, renegade marketers think like their customers but simultaneously imagine a world beyond their customers' own thinking. And then they carefully guide customers on a journey to make that world a reality.

To that end, as you read this book, my hope is you'll read it not just through the practical lens of "How can I change the way I think about marketing?" or "How can I change the way my customers think about my brand?" but simultaneously through the more empathetic lens of "How can I change the way my customers think about themselves?"

After all, renegade marketing is less about creating a deeper business connection and far more about creating a much deeper *human* connection. Because in that world, everyone wins, including marketing.

Enjoy the book.

Brent Adamson
Leesburg, VA
July, 2021

INTRODUCTION

Being a chief marketing officer (CMO) is not for the faint of heart. Your colleagues may claim expertise because they watched an entertaining Super Bowl ad and have no hesitation weighing in on your approach. This is the equivalent of the average person saying, "I balance my checkbook, so I'd like to make some recommendations on our CFO's approach to cash management." And while I'm being a bit smug here, the misguided notion that everyone knows marketing hurts our profession, especially when it goes all the way up to the C-suite. Some of this ignorance is not surprising—considering that less than 20 percent of CEOs come from marketing backgrounds, according to various studies of FTSE 1000 and Fortune 100 execs.

Then there's the issue of expectations. Many of today's CEOs look to their CMOs to build the brand, increase revenue, inform business strategy, and drive differentiation in less than twelve months, regardless of budget, staffing, tech resources, product quality, competitive activity, customer experience, or pricing strategies. In other words, CMOs are expected to be miracle workers and, in the absence of miracles, are distrusted (the *Harvard Business Review* reported in 2017 that 80 percent of CEOs don't trust their current CMOs) and then dismissed (the average tenure of a CMO is between twenty-four and thirty-six months, depending on the study). It's no wonder that only a small percentage of CMOs are satisfied in their roles. Yeah, it's rough out there. And I should know.

I've been on the front lines of this ever-changing business for four decades. My introduction to the creative potential of this industry started at Wells Rich Greene, which was founded by Mary Wells Lawrence, famous for the classic "Plop plop fizz fizz" Alka-Seltzer ads

planes painted in crazy colors. I then moved to
n as the "University of Advertising," where I was
ndamentals of packaged-goods marketing. From
to Chiat\Day, where a blend of account planning
tivity made it the hottest shop of the 1980s. (They
behind Apple's infamous 1984 Super Bowl ad.) These
th...   es were foundational but not exceptional. That came a
bit later.

In 1993, I started a division of Dentsu, which went on to become Renegade, the marketing agency I run to this day. In the intervening decades, Renegade has worked with a wide range of brands—from giants like Arrow, IBM, and Panasonic to tech start-ups like Cvent, Riskified, and Tungsten Network to midsize companies like Case Paper and WorkForce Software. All with one simple goal: to cut through. A goal fulfilled by a relentlessly tested and refined process, one described in detail in this book. Yet Renegade's work with our customers is only half the story.

The other half is the interviews I've been conducting since 2008. Interviews with the coolest and savviest chief marketing officers I could find. More than 425 and counting. Interviews that sustained two-hundred-plus CMO Spotlight columns for *Ad Age* and 240-plus episodes of the *Renegade Thinkers Unite* podcast. Sixty-four interviews became the basis of my first book, *The CMO's Periodic Table*, and at least a hundred inform the book you're about to read. These interviews fed my insatiable curiosity about marketing and marketers. They helped me figure out what separates the good marketer from the great one. They answered the ultimate question: What does it take to be a renegade marketer?

The answer? CATS.

Yes, you read that correctly. CATS. It's an acronym for the top four characteristics of the most successful marketers that emerged from all my interviews: courageous, artful, thoughtful, and scientific. As it turns out, not only are these traits critical to any aspiring marketer's success but they also provide a fabulous framework for the renegade marketer's playbook. Coincidence? Not a chance.

In the pages ahead, you'll meet many of the cooler CATS in marketing and learn the twelve steps to becoming a renegade marketer.

Part I, Courageous Strategy, walks you through a highly refined discovery process that culminates in finding your brand's purpose. Part II, Artful Ideation, details how to build organizational support for a new marketing initiative while establishing your overarching brand story, voice, and design. Part III, Thoughtful Execution, covers how to assemble an effective marketing plan that engages employees, inspires customers, and attracts new ones. Part IV, Scientific Method, provides a critical examination of metrics, marketing technology, and how building a culture of experimentation will drive perpetual growth. And sprinkled along the way, you'll get a handy set of tools you can use to put these ideas into practice for your business.

Together, we're going to be renegade marketers—and it all begins with courage.

PART I

COURAGEOUS STRATEGY

Whenever you see a successful business, someone
once made a courageous decision.

—Peter Drucker

The film crew for *Good Morning America* arrived at about four in the morning. It was the opening day of Comdex, which, in 1996, was the biggest computer show in the world, and *GMA* was there in search of live showstoppers to match the Vegas setting. In one corner of a two-hundred-square-foot blandly carpeted booth loomed a three-ton AMC Hummer, and just below its gargantuan right front tire rested a brand-new laptop. This computer had been flown over from Japan the day before, hand carried by its engineers. To say the engineers were nervous would be like calling a Hummer a Tonka truck.

They weren't the only ones. John Harris, then VP of marketing for Panasonic Personal Computer Company, was pacing on the sidelines wondering if his career was about to be flattened. It wouldn't matter that it had been the agency's idea to run over their new laptop, the Toughbook, with a Hummer on live television. But it was too late now to back out. The correspondent had already started his introduction, and after the Hummer's engine roared to life, the driver put the behemoth in gear and calmly lurched over the magnesium-encased computer. A second later, Harris reached for the computer, powered it up, and demonstrated to the world that the Toughbook lived up to its name. After the interview, Harris turned to his Japanese counterparts and thanked them for their courage and breathtaking engineering skills. His sweat was no longer visible.

The Toughbook arrived with a bang and went on to become the leader in the ruggedized computer market, reaching half a billion dollars in annual sales. The agency behind this stunt was Renegade—which I had founded with the backing of Dentsu in 1993 and eventually owned outright in 2008. There's more to the Toughbook story, as you'll see later in this book, and the lesson in courage from that nail-biting 1996 day in Las Vegas never left me.

Since then, as both a practitioner and chronicler, mustering courage has been proven repeatedly to be an essential prerequisite for successful marketing and marketers. You may not want to put your product through a career-risking torture test like John Harris did, but you will need to run a gauntlet of your own making, one that separates your brand from the sea of sameness.

Steve Jobs had it right. The great ones "think different." They challenge convention. Recognizing this challenge is the easy part. Cutting through isn't. That takes courage. In Part 1 of your journey to become a renegade marketer, we'll explore the notion of courage in three steps. First, we'll help you get into the right state of mind to follow your own path (Chapter 1: Clear Away the Clutter). Then we'll explore what it means to have a truly differentiated position (Chapter 2: Dare to Be Distinct). Finally, we'll help you transform your brand story into something that is not just good for your company but also for the world we live in (Chapter 3: Pounce on Your Purpose).

CHAPTER 1

CLEAR AWAY THE CLUTTER

*Summary: Marketing has become way more compli-
cated but rarely more effective. Be the Marie Kondo of
marketing. Simplicity and focus are your new besties.*

Wasabi. A Japanese root that makes horseradish seem tame. Goes well
with sushi and sashimi. A word that some of you may remember as
"Waaasaabeee" from the 1999 Budweiser ads. Wasabi. Just six letters.
But, with apologies to Emeril, oh, the bam!

In January 2017, two entrepreneurs gathered in a small office in
Boston. They had the kind of conversation the head of marketing,
Michael Welts, had come to expect from his boss, David Friend. It
wasn't planned. David had just wandered in and noticed Michael putting words up on a whiteboard. That's Michael's thing. He loves thinking problems through using whiteboards. And David loves the creative
part of entrepreneurship.

By then, David Friend had already co-founded five companies, all
of which had successful exits. In other words, they had been sold or
gone public, and David had made a lot of money, so much that he could
start companies without an official brand name, without outside fund-
ing. One of the companies David co-founded was Carbonite, now a

publicly traded billion-dollar entity but once just an idea sparked by a couple of accidents back in 2005.

The accidents were not uncommon or life-threatening. Just annoying. First, Friend's daughter's computer crashed and took with it a just-completed term paper, threatening her ability to graduate. Then, Jeff Flowers, Friend's co-founding partner in all five of their earlier companies, had a similar experience when his wife's computer died, destroying their baby pictures. For the two families, these computer accidents were painful. For Friend and Flowers, they were also an inspiration. Why wasn't there an easy way for their family members to back up files? In that moment, the simple idea for Carbonite was born with two words: "easy backup." With the idea in hand, the next challenge for Friend and his co-founders was finding a name.

Friend hates fabricated names. And names with misspellings. And boring names. And names that have the word "tech" in them. And long names. Trying to name a company with Friend is like finding a needle in a stack of needles on a bed of quicksand. The exercise is not AI based. It's not outsourced. It's pure gut with a large dose of caffeine to pick through thousands of options. This approach yielded "Carbonite" in 2006. Easy to spell. Easy to remember. A name that is rock solid. A name with real meaning that evokes a sense of impenetrable security. So, not surprisingly, eleven years later, Friend was eager to take this approach with Michael Welts.

Back to the whiteboard. Welts had penned out a couple of hundred names. And this was the short list. They had reviewed more than a thousand together. Then on that winter day in 2017, they stumbled across the word "wasabi." Bam! Time stopped.

Well, not literally, but Welts does recall it as "a magical moment I'll never forget." Both Friend and Welts knew this *was* the name. Short. Memorable. Distinctive. And spicy. The perfect name for the "hot cloud storage" company they were looking to build.

Backing up a bit, David Friend and his co-founder Jeff Flowers had already made the audacious decision to go after Amazon Web Services (AWS). What gave them the courage? A fundamental belief that they could disrupt the cloud storage market with a clear and profoundly simple value proposition: their service would be one-fifth the cost and six times faster than AWS. No tech-speak. Just plain English. Mix in a provocative name, and you have the recipe for another billion-dollar success story.

In his spare time, David Friend teaches an entrepreneurship class. His first assignment to students with a business idea? Write the billboard copy to describe your company. Get the company promise down to eight words or less. If a student can't do this, if they can't explain the company in a few words that even their grandmothers could understand, Friend tells them to ditch the idea and start again. Keep it simple.

David Friend is one of my heroes. When it comes to CEOs, Friend is a renegade. He is the rare CEO who truly understands the power of a big idea and how a simple yet profound brand story can be baked into the product from the beginning. He freely admits he is not an operations guy. He's the visionary who leaves the day-to-day management to others with that skill set. He uses the complexity of today's world to his advantage, never losing his focus on the big picture. For starters, he clears away the clutter.

WHAT JUST HAPPENED?

Oy, the clutter! And I'm not just speaking about the cacophony of messages your brand is hoping to cut through. We'll get to that. For now, let's focus on your brain and all the wondrous ideas you have this very second. Ideas rich with promise. Ideas accumulated from years of stimuli. Ideas that are undoubtedly translating into action items for yourself and perhaps your business associates. If you're like most marketers, your cranium, like your bedroom closet, is crammed with stuff. Way too much stuff.

In his insight-rich book, *Quantum Marketing*, Mastercard CMO Raja Rajamannar lists twenty-one skills that he thinks CMOs will need to master to be successful. Twenty-one! The fifth of these is the mastery of all the latest "data and digital technologies, as these are the two primary engines that will supercharge marketing into the future." While I can't take issue with the importance of data-driven marketing to all CMOs, I can point out that the increased use of marketing technology (MarTech) is adding to the clutter and complexity without always adding to the bottom line, and we have the research to prove it.

To uncover the truth about the marketer's plight, my company conducted its own research among senior marketers in 2019 and then again in 2020 after the COVID-19 pandemic had begun. The findings were rather startling. First off, 85 percent of the 2020 respondents reported that marketing had become more complicated in the last twelve to twenty-four months. The four biggest culprits? Finding alternatives to in-person events (82 percent), more target audiences (61 percent), more data to sift through (52 percent), and more marketing technology to integrate (49 percent). Interestingly, except for the pandemic-caused need for finding in-person event alternatives, these top drivers of complexity were the same in 2019 and 2020. Importantly, this increase in complexity did not correlate to an increase in effectiveness. These findings alone justify this book. But there's more.

While 70 percent of these CMOs believed their company offers unique products or services, only 38 percent thought their current marketing was substantially different from their competition's. Wait, what? In a nutshell, more than 60 percent of these CMOs were admitting to not fulfilling a fundamental marketer mission: differentiate their brand from the competition. Mind-boggling, right? It seems that marketers have become so caught up in the automation of their messages, creating mountains of content, that they've forgotten the foremost marketing imperative—to cut through.

Our research points to other issues related to clutter and complexity. Only 41 percent of the two-hundred-plus CMOs we surveyed could articulate their brand story in eight words or less. Obviously, these folks were never students of David Friend's. If these CMOs couldn't simplify their brand story down to its barest essence, how could they expect their prospects to be able to remember their brand during an increasingly long purchase cycle? Without a simple story to tell, it is not surprising that just over half of these CMOs report having consistent messages across all communications channels. Consistency, as we will cover in detail later, matters more than ever.

And while 90 percent of the marketers we surveyed believed that employee communications were important to the success of new marketing campaigns, only 9 percent allowed more than two months for these activities. The anecdotal explanation I often hear in my interviews is "Sure, I know we should educate and train employees when we are launching new messaging to the outside world, but we just run out of time." The pattern we're seeing here should be clear enough—most marketers know what they need to do, but they can't quite find the time to do it all as well as they'd like. In other words, their work plates are crowded. They're working harder but not more effectively. They're distracted. There's too much darn clutter.

What these results scream is "Help!" Marketers need help getting aligned with their CEO. Help with setting priorities. Help with crafting differentiated brand strategies. Help with creating marketing campaigns that deliver revenue and build the brand. Help with avoiding the peanut-butter effect and spreading themselves thinly across all possible tasks. In sum, help with *clearing away the clutter*. We can do this, my fellow renegades. Out with complexity. In with focus.

SIMPLICITY WILL SAVE B2B MARKETING

In his biography of Steve Jobs, Walter Isaacson writes: "Ever since Apple's first brochure proclaimed 'Simplicity is the ultimate sophistication,' Jobs had aimed for the simplicity that comes from conquering complexities, not ignoring them. 'It takes a lot of hard work,' he said, 'to make something simple, to truly understand the underlying challenges and come up with elegant solutions.'"

Jobs and other creative pioneers were obviously onto something. Simplicity is very much in vogue these days. We are amply fed slick technologies that promise to "simplify" our lives, but we marketers seem to be going in the opposite direction. We are working more hours, we are taking on more tasks, we are adding more elements to our marketing programs, all at tremendous cost to our personal well-being and, sadly, not to the benefit of our companies either.

The COVID-19 pandemic, which turned the world upside down, surely didn't help. The way we live, play, eat, shop, learn, and, of course, the way we work have changed dramatically. And I firmly believe there's no going back. There will be no "return to normalcy." For example, most likely you will be working from home at least part-time indefinitely. Which means you won't be commuting as much. Which means you'll probably be working even more hours. Wait, what?

Yup, instead of reclaiming your commute time for exercise or education or general wellness activities, we all simply "donated" those hours to our workplaces. It's as if work is the world's largest Electrolux, vacuuming up hours like unwanted dust bunnies. Working from home hasn't blurred the boundaries between our professional and our personal lives; it's obliterated them. Especially for marketers. We marketers have become Energizer Bunnies. We're always on. At least, that's what we tell ourselves when we're responding to emails at two in the morning.

Not surprisingly, a March 2021 study commissioned by software vendor Sitecore revealed that 59 percent of US marketers wanted to quit their jobs at least once in the past year, and 79 percent found the pandemic to be the most challenging time in the history of their careers. It seems that almost overnight the rules of the marketing game changed. As Sitecore CMO Paige O'Neill explains, "Going forward, marketers must accept that this is the new norm, and we aren't going back to where we were before."

Perhaps we need to take a lesson from Japanese organizing guru Marie Kondo, known for her book *The Life-Changing Magic of Tidying Up*, TV appearances, and her Netflix show. Her passion is teaching others how to simplify their lives by purging their homes of unneeded and "joyless" possessions. We can and must do the same with our marketing. Need more evidence?

Consider the work of Brent Adamson, a distinguished vice president at the global research and advisory firm Gartner and author of two groundbreaking books, *The Challenger Sale* and *The Challenger Customer*. Adamson's research foretells even longer sales cycles and more decision-makers, leading to a complex and convoluted buyer's journey. Even well-intentioned efforts by marketers to customize messaging by roles and personas can lead to an inconsistent view of their product or service when the unruly fourteen-person buying committee finally convenes, thus decreasing their chance of closing the deal by two times, according to Adamson's research. As it turns out, brands with clear and consistent messages are far more likely to get the sale than the ones who pursue a matrixed approach to messaging.

Now, I know you might be thinking: *Drew, marketing is never going to be ridiculously simple! That ship has long departed.* I beg to differ.

The first step to building an effective business-to-business (B2B) brand strategy is committing to *clearing away the clutter*. Forget all that you can do and focus on what you must do to make a difference. As time-management coach Elizabeth Grace Saunders explained in a 2020 article on FastCompany.com, "Saying 'no' by either not accepting commitments in the first place or by eliminating commitments that are currently on your plate is your most powerful organizational tool. It's the equivalent of decluttering your closet before you attempt to hang everything up. By reducing the overall number of items, you make it easier to organize. When you 'declutter' from a time-management perspective, you're not only giving yourself less to fit into each day but also more time to keep the whole system maintained."

THE CLUTTER OF MESSAGING

This wouldn't be a marketing book if I neglected to mention the proverbial clutter of brand-related content vying for our attention. It's real. And it's intense. Every second of every minute of every hour of every day is crammed with messages from some brand. It's numbing if not deafening. Consider a few of these clutter-revealing factoids:

- More than 4 million blog posts are published on the internet every day.
- More than 500 million tweets are posted every day.
- More than 5 billion Google searches are made every day.
- About 300 billion emails are sent per day, and that number is expected to reach 350 billion by 2023.
- Facebook Messenger and WhatsApp handle 60 billion messages a day.
- Three hundred hours of video are uploaded to YouTube every minute.
- Despite online ad blockers and TV ad zappers, we are still exposed to thousands of advertisements each day.

That's a lot of content. Content that is meant to grab your attention. Content that is competing for share of mind with your precious brand messaging. And your job as a soon-to-be-christened renegade marketer is to cut through all this noise. To do that, we need to start by *clearing away the clutter*, tightening up our priorities, and focusing our energies like a laser beam on the *must do*, not the *can do*.

Undoubtedly, this takes courage. But as the old saying goes, fortune favors the brave. Let's make your to-do list shorter and more meaningful. Let's not just admire the accomplishments of David Friend, let's internalize his lessons. Let's commit to creating simpler stories not because it is au courant but rather because it is timelessly effective. Let's be renegade marketers.

Clear Away the Clutter Pledge

○ I will focus relentlessly on a handful of strategic priorities.

○ I will have the courage to say no to distractions.

○ I will delegate everything except the things only I can do that move the organization forward.

○ I won't add to my to-do list without taking something off of it.

○ I will block off thirty minutes a day for thinking big.

KEY TAKEAWAYS

- In a time-constrained world, focus is your only friend.
- Give yourself permission to think big and ignore the trivial.
- It takes relentless dedication to keep things simple.

CHAPTER 2

DARE TO BE DISTINCT

Summary: Conformity crushes marketers and marketing. Commodities aren't us. Stand out. Better yet, be unique, inside and out.

Clutter cleared. Now what? Keeping to the basics, we need to focus on how you as a marketer can have a material impact on your brand strategy. Notice that I used the word "brand" and not "marketing" in front of "strategy." That's because, as the marketer, you have an opportunity to transform your entire organization, not just the words and images that are used in your communications. Braced by their courage, this is what the coolest CATS in marketing do. To put it bluntly, the others tend to be packing up their stuff in less than three years without having left a mark.

The CMO role is well known for being the hot spot in the C-suite, the one with the highest expectations and the shortest tenure, and the most varied in terms of responsibilities. Essentially, you have an extremely short period of time to effect change, and that's getting harder, not easier, given all the spending options available to marketers. Thus, the appeal for courage.

Specifically, you need the courage to fight for an overarching brand strategy that differentiates your company. You need the courage to recognize that being unique, or at least distinctive, is more important than being better. Let's chew on this a bit more—your top priority as head of marketing is to help your company stand out from the crowd. Period. Because when you stand out, you create a gravitational force toward your brand. As Aptology CMO Caroline Tien-Spalding explains, "When your brand is different, anyone with that specific need or self-identification will see you as the obvious choice; otherwise, at the next product launch, you are at risk of being caught in the arms race and lose the edge of speed and feed. The costs of the race for features is never ending and expensive from an engineering, timing, and distribution perspective. Branding is a shield that outlasts feature lists." If you can't embrace this challenge, you're probably in the wrong role. Anybody who wants to do effective marketing is probably going to have to take a chance and try something new.

A key part of *daring to be distinct* is recognizing that it's not just enough to have a strategy; you need to understand the notion of uniqueness and what that means. It's not that Ikea is better than Ethan Allen. They're different. Really different. Every aspect of the Ikea experience is unique. If you're marketing Ikea, you're starting with a brand that is fundamentally unique at its core. Lucky you. Most CMOs, especially those on B2B brands, arrive at companies that lack this caliber of uniqueness, having survived despite blending into their crowded markets.

UNIQUENESS IS A CHAIN OF LINKS

In Michael E. Porter's seminal book, *On Competition,* he emphasizes the need for uniqueness in a series of chain links like strategic positioning and operational effectiveness. Ikea is a poster child for this approach, with every aspect of their business, from how their products are made, packaged, and displayed to how employees are trained and rewarded, being unique to that organization and all in service of one clear vision. Since Ikea brings smart design to the masses, their showrooms are in suburbs right off major highways. To keep costs down, everything is designed to minimize store staff, including how the products are displayed and how their loading areas are organized. Even their cafeteria, another unique component, is built around self-service, in a sense training the shopper to make decisions on their own. How can you not admire that? If your organization can get there, chances are you won't need the help offered in this book!

Typically, corporate strategies begin with abstract concepts like mission (what we're doing today), vision (where we want to go), and values (code of ethics). While all of these concepts can be extremely useful, typically they are generic. They're usually boring. They're usually exhaustive. And as such, few in the organization can remember them or, more importantly, are guided by them. It comes back to courage. Crafting a brand strategy in a way that makes the organization unique takes courage. It means not trying to be all things to all people. It means saying no to something. Or, as Steve Jobs put it, "It's only by saying no that you can concentrate on the things that are really important."

In the pages ahead, we'll spend more time on how you can rework your strategic approach to avoid the pitfalls noted above. But first, I thought you'd appreciate a quick story on the power of saying no.

A COURAGEOUS CONTRACTOR

I was one of seven on the board of our cooperative (co-op) apartment building in New York City for fourteen years, and halfway through, we decided to redo the hallways. The carpet, lighting, and wallpaper were showing forty years of wear and tear. None of us on the committee had done a construction project in a co-op before. Three construction companies presented their services. The first informed us they did residences and restaurants. They described their process as starting at the bottom of the building and working their way up.

The second said similar things about doing restaurants and small buildings, condos, and co-ops.

The third came in and informed us that they only did hallways for co-ops and condos. Really? They proceeded to educate us on the need to send a series of ten specific emails to our fellow co-op owners, detailing the process and stages along the way of the project. "And by the way, the biggest complaint in construction of hallways of co-ops is filth, dirt, dust, so we allocate ten percent of our budget for cleaning up every night. And we even use special sanders with vacuums attached to suck up the dust as we go. . . . And we always start at the top and work our way down because gravity is your friend."

As you could imagine, this was the easiest decision ever. After the meeting, I had to ask John Marino, the owner of JMPB Enterprise, how they had arrived at specializing in hallways. He admitted that, at first, it had been terrible to turn down business for other types of jobs, but now, the company is invited to bid on almost every condo and co-op hallway renovation project in New York City, they win 70 percent of their pitches, and they are almost never underbid because they're so efficient. They know their profit margins are higher because they have construction crews they can move from building to building, including door specialists.

A little coda to this story is that our co-op decided not to use JMPB for the door handles and locks because we would save $10,000, and that was the only part of our hallway renovation that went astray!

When you think about developing a distinctive and perhaps unique brand strategy for your business, there are usually three basic dimensions to explore first—what you do, how you do it, and for whom you do it (we'll get to why in the next chapter). In the case of JMPB Enterprise, they were clearly differentiated on both the "who" and "how" dimensions. By working with only co-ops and condos, they evolved how they went about their job to address the major pain points of their customers, specifically dust alleviation. More importantly, from a buyer's standpoint, they changed the way we thought about the project—from having a construction job to complaint mitigation. That is what JMPB was really selling: minimizing apartment owner complaints. And even though John didn't state it that way, "complaint mitigation" was their true point of difference. We had not even thought about complaints, but he was right. We were just thinking about carpets, lights, wallpaper . . . the end state, not the process that would determine a successful outcome. (You may want to read that last sentence again. This is what CMOs really mean when they say you must understand the buyer journey.)

That project was exactly on schedule. Their expertise was so clear. If you do something repeatedly, you should be able to list ten if not twenty things that someone new to your business category would benefit from knowing—in this case, why you start at the top, why you need dust removal as part of your budget, why you vacuum the halls every night, and so on. Focusing on one segment of the market took tremendous courage, but once they were established, everything else fell into place.

A CLOSER LOOK AT POSITIONING STATEMENTS

In the case of JMPB Enterprise, they found a unique position in the marketplace by focusing on whom they served. In doing so, they created operational efficiencies, not to mention genuine expertise, that clearly set them apart from their more generic competitors. This was a business strategy laid down by the CEO. But what happens when the business strategy isn't unique? What's a renegade marketer to do? Here's where understanding positioning really becomes useful.

Most brands, B2B or B2C, are marginally different from their competitors, and it becomes the marketer's job to uncover something distinctive. The exercise many CMOs turn to is often called positioning, which is literally how a brand is different from its self-defined competitive set. Here is a generic positioning template that is used by B2C and B2B brand marketers:

> For (target audience), (brand) is the (frame of reference) that delivers (benefit/point of difference) because only (brand name) is/has (reason to believe).

Applying this approach to our company, Renegade, our positioning statement would be something like: "For innovative CMOs of midsize B2B companies (target audience), Renegade is the only B2B marketing agency (frame of reference) that can guarantee your brand will cut through (benefit) because our clutter-free process really works (reason to believe)." So far, so good. Except not. No employee will be able to remember that line, let alone find inspiration from it. No customer will be able to parrot back that sentence when offering testimonials. And it's even unlikely that a prospect will find such boastfulness compelling enough to investigate further.

Writing a positioning statement is a good warm-up exercise, like calisthenics, but it's not the endgame for renegade marketers. That comes when you land on a few words, preferably eight or less, that transform your positioning into something remarkable. Why eight or less? Our brains. The more words you add, the harder they are to remember. According to McGill University's *The Brain from Top to Bottom* blog, "Many psychology experiments have shown that our short-term memory can hold only a limited number of separate items. The average is about 7 items, plus or minus 2, depending on the individual."

In Renegade's case, we just needed two words: cut through. That's it. It works internally, driving our process, shaping our internal conversations ("Cut the crap!") and how we think about our "product." It works externally because it speaks to the ultimate benefit of working with us and sets an expectation that both our process and our product are efficient and effective. And it helps explain why our logo is a handsaw. It even inspires the premiums we send our clients. That's a lot of communication for just two words. In Chapter 5, we'll give you lots of other examples and even tell you how to create one of your own, but for now, let's return to why this is so important.

Everything in this book comes back to the only commodity that none of us can make more of, which is time. With the paucity of time front and center, you'll want to turn your positioning into a few words your employees can remember and, ideally, use that same language to inspire customers and attract prospects. As the next story reveals, this prescription is about a lot more than just nice words; it's also about actions that back them up.

REPOSITIONING TO FORCE ORGANIZATIONAL CHANGE

In a Gallup poll published in August 2018, the health care industry ranked just above the pharmaceutical industry and the federal government as Americans' three least favorite business sectors. These negative feelings run deep and create a formidable challenge for health care marketers, especially since messaging alone is unlikely to change perceptions.

So, how does a chief marketing officer in the health care industry approach, let alone solve, a gargantuan problem like this?

One CMO responsible for this great challenge was David Edelman, who took the CMO reins at Aetna in 2016 and, a year later, launched the campaign "You don't join us. We join you." In my interview with Edelman, who was abundantly enthusiastic about the organization's transformation, he notes that this was not about a new tagline. Preceded by six months of internal sell-in and significant training, this was Aetna's first unified effort across all its divisions. Outlining the positioning behind the idea along with the critical steps it took to get there, Edelman reports the campaign has had a measurable impact on both employee morale and customer satisfaction.

Aetna qualifies as a huge brand with complex challenges, yet they boiled it down to a relatively simple idea.

When I asked Edelman to describe the premise behind the campaign and how they'd arrived at the chosen statement, he explained, "You don't join us. We join you. We join you in helping you achieve your health ambitions. We took that tagline, and we started to flesh out the implications of it. We created six design principles that would guide anything new that we brought to market. One of them is 'know me.' When somebody calls in, we must know everything they would expect us to know about them. We took that on the road and really helped people on the front line understand what that meant for them in terms of their interactions with customers. We then engaged all the top two hundred and fifty leaders of the company in the same way and had them cascade that down. It led to not just people understanding it and feeling a sense personally of what it means, but also some priority initiatives of tangible changes. That whole process took about six months. We've seen greater employee engagement since then, and that emotional tie has been really powerful for people. This sense of mission is a powerful magnet for people who want to engage in helping to change health care."

You have this new positioning, and then you must deliver. You can't skimp on change management or socialization, which so many big companies do.

Aetna, in contrast, spent six months retraining to make sure that this idea could come to life. Edelman went so far as to establish an "office of the customer" within his department to make sure there were individuals dedicated to keeping and monitoring Aetna's new commitment. This is obviously a very broad view of the role of marketing. And that, too, my friends, takes courage.

In the case of Aetna, *daring to be distinct* inspired a change to the actual service. Experienced marketers have the courage to challenge the status quo. They'll ask for a seat at the product development table, hoping that they can "bake marketing" into the product development process so what comes out of R&D is unique from the outset. These cool CATS have the daring to tap into trends, to find inspiration from unfavorable reviews, and to go out on sales calls to learn firsthand why some deals aren't closing. And some have the daring to start their own categories even when they don't have the massive resources of an Aetna to make it happen. How? Read on, renegade marketers, read on.

CREATE YOUR OWN CATEGORY

Some marketers are in a class by themselves at putting their companies in a class by themselves. These unique individuals are masters of what's called category creation, an approach that takes both courage and diligence. There are many familiar examples of category creation in the MarTech world: inbound marketing from HubSpot, ABM from Demandbase, CRM from Salesforce, and the granddaddy of MarTech, search marketing from Google. But this approach is not limited to marketing technology brands.

Scott Brazina has been through the process of category creation at two companies, PTC (category: product lifestyle management) and Impact (category: partnership automation). In our September 2020 interview, Brazina shares the prerequisites for creating a category. First, explains Brazina, "It really starts with the customer value of the vision." He advises:

> Don't even get started if you're not convinced that the customer value is broad enough, real enough, and

demonstrable. It cannot be a sales pitch. It can't be a
marketing pitch. You've got to be arm-in-arm with
executive leadership and product and say, "Does this
make sense?" You've got to go litmus test it as we did at
PTC and we're doing in spades at Impact. We've been
doing it for a number of years. Litmus test the ideas
with your leading customers and analysts and leading
press that know the space. Let them challenge your
ideas.

The advantage of creating your own category from a differentiation standpoint should be obvious. You set yourself apart. You have
some pricing power. You get to tell your employees they are trailblazers, bringing something new and meaningful to the marketplace. You
get to tell your customers that they, too, are trailblazers, working with
an industry leader. And you get to tell your prospect that you are solving new problems, one's that they will care about once they become
better informed. So far, so good. But there is a catch. Or two.

The first catch is that it's not really a category until you have
competitors, an irony that gives you a potentially short window to
capitalize on your distinctiveness. The second catch is that, in most
cases, you don't get to be the final arbiter when it comes to defining
categories. That falls on the all-important and mercurial sage class
known as analysts. Working at places like Gartner, IDC, Forrester, and
SiriusDecisions (now part of Forrester), analysts issue reports to their
subscribers that compare your brand to those they consider your clos-
est competitors. Given their role as kingmakers, it's no wonder that
most category creators also happen to get chummy with key analysts,
enlightening them on the need for a new class of products/services.

Just in case you're thinking about this approach, you'll want to
bring the industry along, which usually means convening conferences
(many of which went virtual in 2020 but will return to in-person when
the pandemic abates). The trade shows Dreamforce (from Salesforce)
and Inbound (from HubSpot) are two well-established examples. Gabi
Zijderveld, the CMO of AI software company Affectiva, took this
approach, orchestrating the first-ever Emotion AI Summit in 2017, and
followed that up with ones in 2018 and 2019. These events helped to put

Affectiva at the center of an emerging AI software category, attracting $26 million in Series B funding and allowing them to expand into areas like automotive and conversational interfaces.

Going back to the notion that CMOs typically have a limited tenure, one way to extend your stay is to focus on the things that will have the biggest impact on the organization. Affectiva's Zijderveld helped to broaden the markets for her company's software and, in doing so, joined the ranks of courageous growth drivers. And while driving growth is certainly one way to almost guarantee you'll keep your job, there's more to it than that. It's just a lot more gratifying to make a big strategic bet and then help it to pay off.

If any of this sounds risky, good. I worry sometimes that in the telling of these stories after the fact, I gloss over the risks and make it all seem so logical, as if the outcome were all but assured. In the moment, nothing was guaranteed. For example, #EmotionAI could have been ignored or, worse, ridiculed as a superficial effort to ride the AI bandwagon.

In marketing, as in business, I've noticed that the biggest risk is usually not taking one. Netflix made the huge leap to online streaming at the time DVDs were still the dominant media platform. As of January 2021, Netflix has over 200 million streaming subscribers worldwide. Blockbuster, once the dominant player in video rentals, was late to the download party and lost everything. Kodak, which dominated the film category for a century, went bankrupt after failing to find its way in the digital-photography era despite a good twenty years of warning. Yes, these are big strategic fails that no amount of marketing could have prevented, assuming you look at marketing as execution. And that's the point here. Courageous marketers are business strategists first. If they join a company with a problem that marketing alone can't solve, then they need, as my son likes to say, "to put on their big boy pants" and address the bigger challenge at hand. They need to *dare to be distinct.*

DARING TO THINK FIVE YEARS OUT WITH ARROW

In 2012, Arrow Electronics had about the same market capitalization as its nearest competitor, Avnet. Now it is many billions larger. Marketing, led by Rich Kylberg, vice president of corporate marketing and communications, between 2012 and 2019, played an outsized role in the growth of the company and the transformation of its image from a parts distributor to a catalyst for innovation. And not too surprisingly, this story begins with Kylberg's *daring to be distinct.*

In 2012, Kylberg and his team realized that talking about the parts they distributed wouldn't differentiate the brand. Instead, they needed to show what manufacturers could make with these parts if they focused on the future, an idea encapsulated in their tagline, "Five Years Out." But finding a tangible demonstration of this idea took the imagination of a science-fiction writer, the engineering prowess of a rocket scientist, and the dexterity of a race-car driver.

In 2014, Kylberg and company found their showcase with the SAM Car project. While researching its role in building semiautonomous vehicles, the Arrow team met former Indy race-car driver Sam Schmidt, who was paralyzed from the neck down in 2000 after an accident during a practice lap. Schmidt's story was doubly tragic in that his father, also a race-car driver, had been paralyzed after his own accident on the track. With the shared dream of putting Schmidt back into a driver's seat, the Arrow engineers went to work building a vehicle he could control via head movements.

Building such a vehicle was no walk in the park. As each iteration solved one technical challenge, a new one would emerge. Importantly, this was not about creating a self-driving car; this was about giving control of the vehicle back to Sam. Amazingly, the Arrow team did just that, and with each successive improvement, the story became more incredible. Sam took the car for a lap. Sam got the car up to a hundred miles an hour. Sam drove a prerace lap at the Indianapolis 500. He even overcame the torturous curves up to the top of Pikes Peak.

The videos of Sam's journey made me weep, and I suspect they would touch you as well. I was practically blathering when, later on, Schmidt got the first driver's license issued to a quadriplegic enabling him to take his family out in a specially built road vehicle. I wasn't the only one who found the story moving. Arrow employees found a new sense of pride in their organization. Arrow customers appreciated both the goodwill and the tech savvy behind the story. And Arrow prospects had a reason to think about the company in an entirely new way.

Beyond these core audiences, the press found this story irresistible, sharing it around the world in print, in video, and on TV. The impressions generated are in the billions and counting. Arrow also partners with several nonprofits focused on advocating for the disabled, including Conquer Paralysis Now, No Barriers, and Paralyzed Veterans of America. These charitable actions by Arrow show the sincerity of their commitment and the genuine power of *daring to be distinct.* Had Kylberg not tried to do something no one else had done, none of this goodness would ever have occurred.

In this chapter, we've discussed the fundamental need for marketers to grab the strategic reins of their organization and to seek a unique positioning for their organization. And if unique is impossible, to double down on distinctiveness.

At this point, you might ask why I keep letting you off the "unique" hook by giving you "distinctive" as a backup option. Even if you create a category, competitors are likely to copy your efforts on a product or service level, thus diluting your "unique" offering. But remaining distinctive via your marketing, your imagery, your language, and your actions is always within your control.

I've noticed that many of the marketers we talk to hit a plateau. They're doing lots of good practical things, but the pieces are not fitting together. When you read their company's mission, vision, and positioning statements, you don't see anything unique. You don't see distinctive language or visuals. You don't see the principle of "no" involved. You see, "We're all things to all people for all reasons!" That is the opposite of strategy. And the opposite of courage.

With that courageous spirit in mind, let's move on to how defining your brand purpose can be the enduring North Star guiding all our marketing activities.

KEY TAKEAWAYS

- Distinctiveness should be an organizational commitment, not just a marketing one.
- Demonstrate your distinctiveness in both words and actions.
- There is no excuse for not having a distinctive brand.

CHAPTER 3

POUNCE ON YOUR PURPOSE

Summary: Great brands, like great leaders, lead with purpose. Find yours. Commit to it. Make it real. Keep it real.

Even more than a decade later, Simon Sinek is still in the moment. His 2009 book, *Start with Why*, is the standard-bearer for the purpose-driven movement, which urges brands to find their substantive reason for being. Accounting and consulting giant EY has added "purpose" not only to their own brand strategy but also as a distinct consulting practice, helping other organizations to follow their lead. Many other consulting firms and brand strategy firms have done the same. The reason is clear: enlightened consumers and prospective employees want to buy from and work for companies that have a purpose.

According to new research from Accenture, 63 percent of consumers globally prefer to buy goods and services from companies that stand for a shared purpose that reflects their personal values and beliefs and are ditching those that don't. The fourteenth annual Accenture Strategy's Global Consumer Pulse Research, "From Me to We: The Rise of the Purpose-Led Brand," surveyed nearly thirty thousand consumers from around the world to gauge their expectations of brands and companies today. The study found that companies that stand for something bigger than what they sell, that communicate their purpose and demonstrate commitment, are more likely to attract consumers and influence purchasing decisions, which improves competitiveness. *Harvard Business Review* offers a blunter assessment, noting, "Purpose-driven companies make more money, have more engaged employees and more loyal customers, and are even better at innovation and transformational change."

Purpose-driven companies also have a proven advantage in recruiting the next generation of employees, as both Gen Z and millennials have exhibited a strong preference for working at purpose-driven companies. When the pandemic struck and unemployment started to rise, I wondered if purpose would still matter from a recruitment standpoint. Would purpose feel like a luxury just for good times? Would companies be less concerned about culture and values if there were fewer jobs to go around and less pressure to retain employees? As it turns out, the answer to these questions was categorically and emphatically no!

For companies lucky enough to offer cloud-based services, demand skyrocketed and hiring continued unabated. One CMO in the red-hot cloud contact center space mentioned to me at the height of the pandemic that they had forty open positions in their marketing department and filling these positions meant increasing their emphasis on being a more purpose-driven organization. However, even B2B companies that experienced layoffs weren't backing off their purpose-driven efforts, recognizing that they were now asking their remaining employees to do more with less.

What, then, does it mean to *pounce on your purpose*?

BIG *P* AND LITTLE *P*

At Renegade, we tend to think of purpose as falling into two often overlapping categories. There's big-*P* purpose, which usually includes some element of social good. Think Dove's "Campaign for Real Beauty" and Patagonia's expressed mission to "save our planet." Little-*p* purpose relates more to what a product or service does that goes beyond mere functionality. Ben & Jerry's purpose from its start in 1978 was to make ice cream fun again. Kind Snacks' initial purpose was to be "kind" to the body since its founder Daniel Lubetzky couldn't find any healthy snacks during his international travels. Both food brands reach into capital-*P* territory as well, Ben & Jerry's with its advocacy of social justice and ecological preservation, and Kind with its Kind Foundation to "foster kinder and more empathetic communities."

While the above examples of purposeful strategies are for consumer brands, rest assured purpose is also a rapidly growing consideration for business-to-business companies. Global software giant SAP is but one of many examples of converts to the purpose movement. In our 2019 podcast interview, Alicia Tillman, then SAP's CMO, explains, "Businesses today are in the business of making the world a better place regardless of what you do or the industry you're in or the products and the services that you deliver." Understanding this, Tillman and company evolved their stated purpose to "help the world run better and improve people's lives" and modified their tagline from "the best-run companies run on SAP" to "the best-run companies make the world run better."

This may seem like a subtle change, but the organizational implications for SAP have been substantial. Explains Tillman, "It's all about making something better. And in a lot of cases, it's about making the environment better, our economy better, society better. And that was the fundamental change that we made which is, how do we really help our customers achieve their ultimate vision which is to make the world run better. And so that's the change that we made."

HOW BANK OF THE WEST PAID FOR ITS PURPOSE

One reason so many marketers are enamored with "starting with why" is that, chances are, your "why" is going to be unique relative to your "what" and "how." Let's take banks, for instance. The financial industry is highly regulated, making product uniqueness next to impossible. That's why so many banks look to non-product-related sources for their positioning (like TD Bank, "America's Most Convenient Bank," or HSBC, "The World's Local Bank"). Banks are also interesting to scrutinize because most operate in both business-to-business and business-to-consumer environments. Here's one bank that really went out on a limb with its purpose.

In our revealing podcast interview "The Keys to Effective, Purpose-Driven Marketing," Bank of the West's chief marketing and communications officer, Ben Stuart, explains his purpose-driven brand. "Society is changing. Entrepreneurship is changing. The face of youth is changing. The face of leadership is changing. Energy is changing. The environment is changing. And you need a bank to keep up with the pace of change for a planet that is in a constant state of change. That's why we're 'the bank for a changing world.'"

Recognizing the change is one thing, and embracing the change is yet another, especially when it means changing how and with whom you do business. Stuart continues, "Most of the language of banking is bankrupt, including the subject of sustainability. We need to talk about specifics, like our investments in the community, diversity, and renewable energy. Real things, real commitment. So, Bank of the West spent energy talking about what sets them apart; they will not finance tobacco, coal-fired power plants, fracking wells, or certain types of palm oil if it's not harvested correctly, which is fundamentally different from the competition."

This purposeful approach took courage. A lot of courage, given the sharp teeth of their new positioning. Initially, Bank of the West put its money where its mouth was and divested upward of a billion dollars in assets that had been going to areas misaligned with the brand's purpose. Clearly, this bank took to heart Michael E. Porter's words, "The essence of strategy is choosing what not to do." On the flip side, Bank of the West has enjoyed significant growth in other business areas, particularly in its two biggest states, California and Colorado. As noted earlier, it takes courage to identify and stick to a distinctive brand strategy, particularly one that is purpose driven.

Many B2B companies, even category leaders, find it hard to keep their products, services, or processes distinctive. Competitors flock to success like fleas to a dog. They study and try to copy what you do and how you do it. But what they can't do is copy your "why," especially when it becomes ingrained in every aspect of the organization. When that happens, watch out. Employees are more engaged, and customers are more loyal. And prospects notice.

STANDING FOR SOMETHING: STATE STREET GLOBAL ADVISORS

Stephen Tisdalle, the CMO of State Street Global Advisors, joined the third-largest asset manager on the planet in 2016 with a definite agenda in mind. As he explains: "I had said in taking this role, we either are going to fit in the category or we're going to lead. We've done a great job in fitting in the category since our inception over forty years ago. But if we're going to lead the category, we're going to have to make some bold statement, and have real conviction, and that has to be evidenced in the way we communicate." And girl, did they communicate!

Recognizing that public companies with women on the board of directors outperformed companies with all-male boards, State Street created an exchange-traded fund with the trading symbol SHE. The SHE fund was a unique idea at the time, one that begged for an equally distinctive marketing campaign, assuming State Street had the courage to take a stand.

They did. Revealing the *Fearless Girl* statue on March 7, 2017, which not coincidentally was also International Women's Day, this fifty-inch bronze beacon became an international phenomenon, generating billions of social media impressions in a matter of hours. Initially permitted for just one week, Change.org took it upon themselves to petition for an extended stay, gathering 2,500 signatures in forty-eight hours! The statue of this brave young girl facing down Wall Street's famous charging bull held its place for another twenty-one months before moving to a permanent location across from the New York Stock Exchange in December 2018.

This was not a vacuous stunt. State Street Global Advisors had a distinct story to tell about fostering greater diversity in the financial industry, a story that ended up having far more impact both externally and internally than anyone could have imagined. After State Street's letter-writing campaign appealing to the largest public companies in the world, more than three hundred of them added women to their boards. Even countries like Japan, which had almost no female representation at the board level, responded with more than twenty-five companies changing their director gender mix.

Pouncing on your purpose is not without its risks. After the *Fearless Girl* installation made headlines globally and generated more than 6.5 billion social media impressions in its first year, a potentially harsh spotlight was turned on State Street about its own levels of diversity. Recognizing they, too, could do a better job in this area, the company faced the challenge head-on, not unlike the statue itself, and made changes to its leadership teams and overall employment practices.

Among the many lessons for renegade marketers offered by State Street's *Fearless Girl* program is that you don't need to tell your whole story in each campaign component. Ironically, the statue is completely silent and only a small plaque accompanies the little bronze girl. In fact, her silent strength speaks volumes. It also sparks questions and conversations that ultimately lead inquiring minds back to State Street, the company's SHE fund, and related diversity-driving initiatives.

Fearless Girl may have remained a simple statue getting her fifteen minutes of fame if it hadn't been for State Street's purposeful actions that reinforced the story she symbolized. They committed to increasing the gender diversity in their own company, as well as encouraging public companies to do the same. Tisdalle explains that "authenticity is attractive" and that people are drawn to marketing campaigns that are aligned with important values. He continues by suggesting that companies and leaders need to "do well, do better, by doing good." And while State Street found a big-*P* purpose to drive their business, there are many occasions when little-*p* purpose can get the job done.

LITTLE-*P* PURPOSE THAT TAKES A PUNCH

In 1994, the nascent computer division at Panasonic invited Renegade to pitch their new laptop computer with a forgettable name, the CF-41. The client was understandably proud of the fact that this was the first laptop with a built-in CD-ROM drive. Up until that moment, business professionals who took their laptops with them on business trips also had to carry around a bunch of accessories, including a separate CD-ROM drive.

Thinking that these individuals were like a one-man band carrying all of this stuff around, for the pitch presentation, we actually hired a one-man band to show up at Panasonic's headquarters in Secaucus, New Jersey. He made a lot of noise, simultaneously pounding his drum, strumming his guitar, and blowing his harmonica. Quickly realizing the client wasn't all that amused, we sent him packing. We won the business despite the silliness of our stagecraft because the client appreciated the thinking behind it. The CF-41 helped eliminate most of the accessories travelers had to haul. For the launch, we created a campaign using illustrations of both the problem and the solution. This approach worked for about a year, but as we got to know the end user better, we realized something else—these folks thought of themselves as road warriors and were often in situations that put their laptops at risk of damage. Instead of focusing solely on the multifunctional characteristics of the CF-41, we could shine a light on the fact that it was encased in magnesium, making it significantly more rugged than your average laptop. This led us to a campaign called "Own the Road," in which we made the case that the Panasonic CF-41 was the Hummer of laptops. Importantly, this also helped us turn a negative (the magnesium case added a couple of pounds in weight) into a positive (much more durable) and identified a clear and enduring purpose for Panasonic notebooks—protect mission-critical work.

It was at this point that the product really started to gain traction, and we suggested to Panasonic that they create a truly ruggedized notebook, one that could withstand any kind of abuse. They agreed and came up with the CF-25, which included waterproofing features and a shock-mounted hard drive. Seeing a big opportunity, in 1996, Panasonic asked us to come up with a name, which we did— the Toughbook. Now, both the positioning and the product were fully aligned behind a clear purpose. The name was both the purpose and the promise. From then on, Renegade's job was to bring that purpose to life. And we did just that.

As I mentioned in the introduction of this section, we launched the Toughbook at Comdex, then the largest computer trade show in the world, at which our client had the courage to invite *Good Morning America* to witness live having a six-thousand-pound Hummer drive over the first Toughbook. The laptop survived with a slightly cracked but fully functional screen, much to the relief of its engineers, generating remarkable buzz in the industry.

In the next two years, working closely with the Toughbook marketing team, we orchestrated one of the first online user-generated content campaigns asking the purposeful questions: "How did your notebook die?" and "How did you feel when your notebook died?" We set up drop tests of competitive product at trade shows, creating "graveyards" of dead laptops. We also commissioned IDC to measure how much notebook deaths cost businesses (turns out the figure was more than $750 million per year!). And while Renegade picked up a couple of Effie Awards for marketing effectiveness, thanks to our client's courageous choice of names and highly focused sales and marketing activities, the Toughbook line of laptops soon exceeded $500 million in annual sales.

BEING DISTINCTIVE ON PURPOSE: UTAK

Drug testing in toxicology laboratories must be precise and uncompromisingly controlled. Utak manufactures controls that enable these labs to calibrate the accuracy of their testing equipment. What Utak does is serious. It's also highly technical. Here's how CMO Matt Kopp explains it: "We take human biological matrices like blood, urine, serum, oral fluid, and we take certain drugs, and we actually put those drugs into the matrix at known concentrations, and so laboratories use that material (called controls) to make sure their instruments are calibrated properly." Stay with me, it's about to get simply freaky.

A few years ago, this California-based family-owned company started to bring a little fun and attitude to an otherwise staid industry. Utak did this initially by having a lot of brightly colored swag emblazoned with the words "Control Freaks." Explains Kopp, "It's been something that people really connect with especially since there's not a lot of personality in the clinical world, but it was never the main focus of our marketing."

Sometimes your big idea is right in front of you, and that certainly was the case with Utak. They didn't realize the value of the fun slogan on their T-shirts. Unique to the company and to the category, "Control Freaks" became more than just a line on a T-shirt; it became the company's rallying cry, their reason for being, and what we call their purpose-driven story statement. Utak employees are both literally and figuratively control freaks. They are freakishly committed to manufacturing the best controls for laboratories, which, in turn, gives their customers more control.

Importantly, Kopp recognized that "Control Freaks" couldn't be "just that nice tagline." Instead, he explains, "It's really taking ownership of everything that we do no matter what the task is—if it's in manufacturing extremely complex controls, dealing with drugs and all the mathematics and chemistry, or processing orders through our ERP system, or just shipping a box out, it is being focused and really being a control freak about that process, like double-checking work, looking at stuff to make sure it goes out perfect."

From an employee standpoint, "Control Freaks" became about quality control promised and delivered. Employees are now rewarded based on their commitment, and high performers are recognized as "Control Freaks of the Month." Potential recruits are being screened for the requisite "compulsive" tendency. Kopp even went so far as to change his title to "Chief Control Freak," sending a clear and unexpected message both internally and externally.

To make this idea resonate even further with customers, Utak evolved its packaging with the idea of tangibly giving the company more control over its controls. By making it easier for lab technicians to add their own usage dates to the packages, since these chemical mixtures are often used intermittently, Utak helped labs be control freaks too.

For prospective customers, Utak looked to gain more control over its digital presence, updating the company's website with the "Control Freaks" promise and optimizing content for the search engines. Known in the industry as SEO, for search engine optimization, this was a key step in helping Utak be discovered by new clients. Kopp notes, "We've seen a huge increase in web traffic just by focusing on what we were doing tactically in the digital marketplace."

All these highly focused activities helped Utak exceed its sales goals and build a strong platform for future success. It didn't happen overnight. Kopp advises his fellow CATS, "Don't drift, stay true to the plan, it's going to take a long time and you have to follow it through."

Kopp and his team have a purpose-driven strategy that, by design, changed the entire organization, made easier by a plan that fits on one page.

That's right, one page. For Utak, that means eighteen "Control Freaks"–related ideas, six for each of their core targets, employees, customers, and prospects, all outlined on a single page. Granted, some of the details are missing, but all the essential elements are there, including goals, metrics, and key tactics. One story, three targets, one page, clear metrics. Now that's *clearing away the clutter*!

KEY TAKEAWAYS

- A well-articulated brand purpose can differentiate your brand and provide the connective tissue for all your marketing activities.
- You don't have to promise to save the world to have a meaningful brand purpose.
- It's not enough to define your purpose; you must take action to make it real.

PART II

ARTFUL IDEATION

None of us is as smart as all of us.

—Ken Blanchard

Courage is essential, but as marketing leaders, we can rarely order an organization to shift gears or insist that the target audience buy our product or service. We aren't military generals who can command soldiers to take the hill. Instead, we renegade marketers need to be cleverer, even in how we apply the multiple meanings of the word "artful." We need to be artful communicators, internally and externally. And we need to embrace artfulness when it comes to the design of our brands. The good news is that with all your newfound courage, artful ideation will seem like a perfectly pleasant picnic.

In Chapter 4: Welcome We, artful applies to your ability to build consensus around a big idea. In Chapter 5: Perfect Pithy, we're going to challenge you to artfully articulate your brand story in eight words or less. And in Chapter 6: Delight by Design, we'll explore the fundamental importance of design, from the look and feel of every aspect of your brand to how you design your brand story. Along the way, you'll meet some artful CATS who were kind enough to share their anything but "purrfect" marketing journeys.

CHAPTER 4

WELCOME WE

Summary: Marketing is best played as a team sport. Involve your organization top to bottom early and often. Share the credit and the gear.

John Costello, the former CEO and CMO of Dunkin Brands, shared a maxim to a large gathering of CMOs that I'll never forget. Quoting Harry Truman, among others, Costello said, "Anything is possible if you don't care who gets credit." This is great counsel for any person in any situation, but it is particularly important to marketing leaders. In truth, we marketers alone can't drive the type of organizational change that is often required for marketing initiatives to be effective. We need a lot of help from a lot of other departments.

In this chapter, we'll provide numerous real-world examples of what happens when a CMO shifts from a "me" to "we" perspective. Before we get there, here are three action items for any CMO, especially those of you who've just started at a new company:

1. **Befriend your HR leader:** Work with them to *engage employees first* (see Chapter 7). Field an employee survey upfront to benchmark attitudes about the company and

to gather feedback on the brand itself. The survey sends a signal to employees that you care about "we."

2. **Befriend your CFO:** Work with them to help *measure what matters* (see Chapter 10). Teach them about the inclusive power of marketing, that we can't just measure leads and revenue. Have them teach you about the financial mechanics of the organization. Every marketer needs to understand how a company makes money.

3. **Befriend your head of sales:** Start by going on a sales call as an observer, but then do a sales presentation on your own. Your sales chief will appreciate your effort to walk in his or her shoes. From there, you can start to break down any sales-versus-marketing tension. Marketing is hard enough without this unnecessary yet age-old conflict.

Being an artful communicator, whether you're communicating internally or externally, requires a timeless skill that makes a lasting impression: listening. My father, Carl Neisser, who continued working well into his eighties as a masterful connector, believes that listening is his true superpower and mainly a lost art. (By the way, he was also kind enough to share what he'd learned from nine decades as an artful communicator in episode one hundred of *Renegade Thinkers Unite*.) In our world of renegade marketing, I'm so happy to say that curiosity does not kill the cool CATS—it makes us stronger!

DARA ROYER, MERCY CORPS—NOT ENOUGH TO BE RIGHT

Dara Royer's journey as chief development and marketing officer of Mercy Corps is profoundly instructive for all businesses, especially those with modest budgets and massive expectations. Mercy Corps's rebranding increased awareness, revenue via donations, and recognition by the Harris Poll as the 2017 EquiTrend Brand of the Year and Most Loved Brand in the category of International Aid Nonprofits. Those are results that would delight any chief marketer. But how the heck did Royer and her team accomplish so much with so little?

Ultimately, the key takeaways from Royer's rebranding efforts can be seen as a mini-marketing plan spelling out frugality, storytelling, and leadership. For starters, Royer took the idea of DIY, or do-it-yourself, to a whole new level in her rebranding efforts. Wanting to develop a solid strategic foundation for rebranding, Royer knew that conducting research would be invaluable. The only problem was cost. Typically, a global study involving hundreds of interviews can cost more than a hundred thousand dollars, money her organization did not have.

So, what did Royer do? She made sure her marketing team was trained in research methodology and equipped them with the communication skills to work with their field organization, government officials, and the beneficiaries of Mercy Corps's work. By dedicating that time and energy to training the marketing team and the field staff, they were able to produce consistent and valid results that allowed specific themes to emerge and guide their rebranding efforts. Involving the organization in the research had the added advantage of making all the key stakeholders feel like owners of both the process and the ultimate outcome.

Once the research was concluded, Royer drafted a clear strategy statement that focused on telling an epic story that would work across forty-two countries and a broad array of cultures. With this strategy in hand, Royer focused on telling emotionally charged stories that resonated with all stakeholders, including employees, donors, and those affected by Mercy Corps actions.

Royer found that the toughest lesson she had to learn when it comes to rebranding is that having strong hunches early on doesn't matter. When she suggested a direction to her peers near the outset of the research, this idea was dismissed, not because it was invalid but simply because she hadn't taken the time and effort to gain their buy-in. Marketing is a team sport, and the players must believe in and feel part of your plan. Even if you think you have the big idea, you can't just expect a large organization to fall in line. Consensus building is an art form that must be mastered for any enlightened leader to succeed. Fortunately for Royer, the necessity of conducting the research in-house had the added benefit of involving many employees in the process, making the ultimate adoption of the new brand positioning less of a sales effort and more of a "look what you all helped create" success story.

Like Royer, David Edelman of Aetna, whom you met in Chapter 3, also acknowledged the critical need to *welcome we*. In his six-month campaign of creating new internal and external language, Edelman noted that his biggest lesson learned was that building consensus through the rebranding process had been essential. He thought he had the answer early on, yet found organizational resistance to his idea. It wasn't until Edelman did extensive research involving employees, customers, and prospects was he able to build consensus around their big new story.

WELCOMING WE INCLUDES VALUES

Denise Broady, currently CMO at Appian, and CMO and COO at WorkForce Software from 2015 to 2020, knows plenty about both core values and adversity. Having fled Vietnam as a child, Broady learned to become resilient while growing up as an "outsider" in Richmond, Virginia.

When Broady arrived at WorkForce Software in 2015, she noticed that the core brand values had not been clearly defined. Working with the leadership team, she made this her top priority. Changing the heart and soul of this established international company, with employees spread out across the globe, was no easy feat. That didn't stop Broady from helping to redefine WorkForce's ideology from the inside out.

In our podcast interview, Broady explained how she helped construct WorkForce's values and drive its future success: "Coming in, it was tough to even look at the company and say, 'Wow, we don't even have core values.'" Given the go-ahead from her CEO to take the initiative, she isolated three key areas: putting the customer first, making things happen, and celebrating success. "Imagine taking these three principles, going out with a small team, getting twenty-five people to sign off and endorse it, and then rolling it out to the entire company," recalls Broady. "When you have to come in and actually change people's perspective on something so fundamental as core values, it's not an easy task," she explains.

To make this happen, Broady first assembled a committee of twenty-five senior execs from across the organization, including HR, sales, finance, product development, operations, customer service, and, of course, marketing. The management committee's initial task was to identify a range of core value concepts that were then winnowed down to three. Then they had the job of fleshing these out in a series of workshops with more employees directed by individual members of the committee. The workshops helped strengthen the language and ensure that the values would be accepted by the broader organization. From there, the values were introduced at a companywide event in the United States and then dispersed internationally via a video and explanatory booklet.

Broady recommends not rushing through this type of work, recalling, "We didn't roll out the core values until a year after I was at WorkForce Software." Listen for the artfulness in her justification for a patient values makeover: "You've got to really feel what the company is about because it needs to be authentic, and it needs to be adopted by every single employee." Broady adds, "Because we're globally distributed, we also need to make sure everybody in the UK feels the same, that everybody in Australia feels the same, and also Livonia, Michigan, and then all the remote folks."

What did Broady conclude after going through this extensive values-generation process? "I always tell my team it's not about being integrated to sales; it's about being integrated to the business."

WELCOMING WE PROVIDES A CLEAR PATH TO PURPOSE

Cofense is in the cybersecurity space, providing a platform that helps companies defend themselves against phishing attacks. Launched in 2008 as PhishMe, the company was the first to provide training programs that simulated phishing attacks, helping employees to recognize and then report suspicious-looking emails. These nefarious emails are responsible for a huge percentage of security breaches leading to all sorts of problems like malware, ransomware, and identity theft.

With an expanded suite of services and new private equity investors, PhishMe changed its name to Cofense in early 2018. This is often a pivotal moment for any start-up, and the brand launch ran into some hiccups as aggressively priced competitors entered the space. Regrouping in 2019, CMO Kevin Fliess was tasked with relaunching the Cofense brand, with the express desire of unleashing a purposeful story.

Welcoming the input from employees via an employee survey and from the executive team via one-on-one interviews, Fliess paved the way for the broad acceptance of a new direction for the company. Applying the methodology detailed in this book (full disclosure: Fliess worked with Renegade on the rebranding), it became clear in the discovery process that Cofense had an amazingly collaborative culture and a genuine commitment to helping clients and the world at large defend itself from insidious phishing attacks.

It also had a platform that became even more powerful as new customers joined the network. With 20 million daily users already reporting suspicious emails and a Phishing Defense Center monitoring and nullifying the impact of cybercriminals, Cofense was ready to rally employees, customers, and prospects around a profound purpose.

Expressed as "Uniting Humanity Against Phishing," Cofense's purpose-driven story statement is simple but not simplistic. These four words both ground the company in its business segment and elevate the company with a reason for being. The statement also begs the audience to ask how. As we saw earlier with State Street's *Fearless Girl* statue, you don't have to tell the whole story in each execution so long as you trigger curiosity.

Ultimately, we marketers *welcome we* because of the occasionally maddening reality that marketing is best played as a team sport. We need employee and customer input to understand where the brand is and where it could be, and employee buy-in to execute effectively. And to get that input and buy-in, we need HR to partner with us, which is exactly what Kevin Fliess achieved with the Cofense HR team. He also spent a lot of time with the customer service team to get a real-time understanding of product performance, making sure that some of that customer feedback resulted in opportunistic product enhancements.

Importantly, the notion of *welcome we* also extends to the greater "we" of customers, so it shouldn't be much of a surprise that Cofense launched their "Uniting Humanity Against Phishing" campaign at their annual user conference in September 2019. With a couple hundred of the company's top customers gathered in Orlando, the event kicked off with a dynamic video inviting Cofense customers to unite in the fight against phishing. It was a powerful "goose bumps moment" for Fliess and company, and just the beginning as they rolled out their we-grounded and we-centric story.

Welcoming we is a necessary step for any CMO who hopes to transform their entire organization via daring strategic moves and purposeful storytelling. The value of this collaborative approach is evident when we look at the longer-than-average tenure of transformative CMOs. Chances are you will stay longer than twenty-four months at your company, thus have the opportunity to drive lasting organizational change, if you move *welcome we* up on your list of priorities. Just consider the case of Kathy Button Bell.

Kathy Button Bell joined Emerson Electric as CMO in 1999 and, as of my writing this book, is still in her role. That's the longest tenure of any of the more than four hundred CMOs I've interviewed in the last decade. Heck, it's the longest I've ever heard of for any CMO. As one frame of reference, consider that among the sixty-four executives featured in my first book, less than half of those were still in the same role just two years after the book came out. Many of the CMOs I've interviewed have had four or more jobs in the last decade. It's worth noting that in that same time frame, Emerson has gone through multiple acquisitions and divestitures, so don't fret about Bell's possible boredom. That was never an issue. Instead, let's dive into what enabled her unrivaled longevity.

Kathy Button Bell is nothing if not a team player. As she explains it, "I don't really want to be the wheel, I like being the cog in the wheel." Not wanting to be known as the "advertising girl," Bell focuses instead on helping to "drive the culture in a positive healthy way," which she insists is "the most fun part of my job." Sensitivity to the business cycle is part of Bell's approach to culture change. She explains, "When business is good, you have to take huge advantage of that moment to fill the organization with optimism. If they're at a jog, try to get them to run. You always want to accelerate positive change."

And what about the downtimes? Can you still afford to *welcome we*? Bell, not surprisingly, responds in the affirmative. Recalling a time of "transformational tension as we shrunk the company before we grew again," Bell sought employee input, and 13,999 responded, informing leadership on "the three things that we were made out of, and the four things we need to do better to be successful." The best part of this process, exclaims Bell, is "they wrote their own plan." *Welcome we*, indeed.

KEY TAKEAWAYS

- Brand transformation begins inside the organization.
- Being right won't get you to the finish line unless you bring your organization along with you every step of the way.
- Artful CMOs recognize they can't succeed without making allies and sharing credit.

CHAPTER 5

PERFECT PITHY

Summary: Find your eight-word story first. Then touch souls with your distinct voice. Edit everything. Get to sparse before sprucing up your copy.

It was an unforgettable moment in a rather eventful career. Scribbling four words on my ruled yellow pad on the first day of a two-month strategic engagement, I knew I had the creative answer to the challenge at hand.

The four words I jotted down that day were "Where Family Comes First," perhaps the best tagline I've ever written. The story of these words, which graced the binder of *Family Circle* magazine for eighteen years until its demise at the end of 2019, illustrates how the promise and potential of everything that marketing could be and, dare I say, should be, is lost.

When we presented this string of words to *Family Circle*, we suggested that it was more than a clever tagline; it could be the glue that held together communications to all the magazine's targets, including employees, advertisers, and readers. We believed the magazine had permission to take a stand, to be the family-first publication. It would just need to go all in. Like moving the family section of the magazine to the front. Like holding family-first symposiums for advertisers, editors, and subscribers. Like offering employees the most family-friendly leave policy in the industry. Like convening writers and advertisers for an annual TED-like confab on changing the meaning of family. Like launching an annual study on what it means to put family first. Put all this together, and you have the makings of a purpose-driven program that's not just unique but also sure to cut through.

However, at that moment, *Family Circle* was not interested or seeking a purpose-driven marketing program. This was a few years before Simon Sinek inspired brands to "start with why" and become focused on brand purpose. And this was also when the word "family" had taken on political connotations, which didn't help. Initially, the magazine staff asked us to explore other lines and ideas, but none made it past their legal department's trademark searches. With no other viable options, they approved the line and shortly thereafter placed it on the magazine spine.

As I said earlier, "Where Family Comes First" is perhaps the best tagline I've ever written, but it comes with a big asterisk, like Roger Maris's record-setting home run season memorialized in the movie *61**. We never had buy-in from the organization that truly effective marketing is not just the veneer of a cleverly crafted promise like *Where Family Comes First* but, instead, a series of actions—such as the ones described above—that make a promise like this real.

MAKING THE CASE FOR CASE PAPER

In the case of *Family Circle*, a clever tagline remained just that: a tagline, a few words for the masthead and the company letterhead and nothing more. To *perfect pithy*, you must create a purpose-driven story statement. These profoundly powerful phrases of eight words or less are far more than a clever tagline. Done artfully, these carefully crafted words represent an organizational promise, a purposeful commitment to all stakeholders, as shown in our next example.

Founded in 1944, Case Paper is still a family-owned business. In fact, their CMO Simon Schaffer-Goldman also happens to be the grandson of the founder, while Simon's dad is the CEO. Quaint, right?

In an industry (paper distribution) marked by consolidation, digital disruption, and massive transformation, Case's durability and ownership structure are certainly distinctive and more than admirable. But the question we asked when Renegade first started working with Simon back in 2018 is why: Why does this history matter? Why did you join the company? Why do your more than four hundred employees in seven different states come to work each day? Why do your customers keep coming back for more paper and packaging materials year after year?

To answer these whys and ultimately help Case articulate its brand purpose, we needed a deeper understanding of what the company did, how it did it, and whom it served. Carrying a massive inventory of paper in warehouses also stocked with converters that could resize giant rolls into customized orders, Case's "what" and "how" were closely aligned with the needs of their customers. Obviously, printers need paper to print. What's not obvious is that printers have faced a perfect storm of declining demand, the expectation of near-instant gratification, and diminished margins. Just to survive, printers needed to find any means they could to increase efficiency. So Case, with its inventory and converters, was well positioned structurally to help printers minimize their overhead and maximize their ability to respond quickly to incoming orders.

The remaining question then became: How do we translate this structural advantage into a meaningful and memorable articulation of purpose? In its more than seventy-five years of selling paper, Case always maintained a customer-first mentality. It was well known in the industry for doing more than expected and reacting unflinchingly to unexpected, sometimes outrageous, requests. It lived by three basic operating principles: be reliable, be resourceful, and be responsive. In sum, Case Paper is and always has been "on the case."

Just three words, but, oh, the power. Suddenly, everything Case was already doing had an easy-to-remember articulation. And looking ahead, Case now had a rallying cry to hold together all future marketing activities. Today, employee evaluations request examples of going above and beyond the call of clients. A new quarterly awards program recognizes employees who are "on the case." Case also shared its purpose externally, first by celebrating printers who are "on the case" for their customers via an annual awards program.

Since putting your customers first and existing to serve are neither new nor distinctive ideas, it's important to understand one other element of "on the case" as a statement of purpose and perfection of pith. It's a pun. And it became even more so when the words "on the" were heretically placed above the word "case" in the Case Paper logo, which then appeared on business cards, email signatures, and CasePaper. com. Now the brand was literally and figuratively on the case. Here, too, we were pulling from the past, as Case Paper had a long history of using whimsical humor in its marketing. Being on the case is good, and doing it in a likable manner in the generally humorless world of business marketing is outstanding. And standing out—or, as we like to say, cutting through—is the true power of pith.

Many CMOs ask, "What's the difference between a tagline and a purpose-driven story statement?" Both "Where Family Comes First" and "on the case" qualify as promising taglines, but only one of these was and is used as an expression of purpose in that Case Paper is taking numerous actions to make the promise of these three words real. To clarify this subtle but important distinction, a purpose-driven story statement leads, if not requires, a brand to do new things internally and externally. A tagline is often a clever but unfulfilled promise.

Purpose-driven story statements are the guiding light for employee engagement programs, customer retention initiatives, and new customer acquisition endeavors. To further illustrate the difference between a tagline and a purpose-driven story statement, here are several examples of phrases from SurveyMonkey, NI, and Command Alkon that could, with a few more actions, blossom into fully integrated B2B marketing programs.

SURVEYMONKEY: POWER THE CURIOUS

Most likely you're one of the many millions who have either completed a survey or fielded one on SurveyMonkey's nearly ubiquitous platform. Awareness is not their issue, noted CMO Leela Srinivasan in our 2019 interview. Since joining the company in April 2018, her goal has been to inspire usage overall and increase adoption of their enterprise-level services. Getting there meant expanding upon the brand's "power the curious" promise by making it real on multiple levels.

To do this, Srinivasan first focused on her internal audience, encouraging employees to create their own surveys, as well as surveying employees for feedback on how to make the company stronger. She also orchestrated a Curiosity Conference, bringing users together to talk about the vital importance of curiosity, not just to marketers but to society. In our podcast conversation, we discussed more ways to make "power the curious" real, like conducting an annual study on curiosity itself, especially since incuriosity seems to be on the rise.

NI: ENGINEER AMBITIOUSLY

Carla Piñeyro Sublett's agency, Gretel, was hired by National Instruments in 2019 with a specific mandate: rebrand the forty-year-old company. Sublett, who went on to become CMO of IBM in 2021, explains, "The problem at hand was that no one really knew who we were or understood what we did, and we had very little awareness." Dear reader, please stop and read the preceding sentence again. What she's describing is the absence of marketing! This doesn't happen by accident and usually signals a deeply rooted operational preference for being product led or sales led or, in the case of National Instruments, engineering led. Solving this problem is not just about finding a few clever words (although that helps); it takes a commitment to change the entire organization.

This understanding was part of Sublett's pitch from the get-go. She recalls, "When I was asked to do the work, one of the things that I said to the CEO and to the board and to the president of the company was, 'Are you prepared to look into the mirror? Because the research may reveal some questions that need to be answered that we haven't answered yet strategically or may reveal some market opportunities.'"

And as it turns out, that's exactly what happened.

Sublett's agency, Gretel, presented two positioning options, and she recalls them saying, "One is very rooted in who you are, and it feels safe and it's comfortable, and the other one is rooted in your heritage, but is actually a big bold step into the future." The company chose the one that challenged its safe strategy. Six months later, this strategy was synthesized into two words, "engineer ambitiously." To an outsider, these two words answer the questions of what NI does (this rebranding included abbreviating the name National Instruments) and why it exists (to tackle the biggest engineering challenges of the day). To an employee, this language signals an end to a "very humble culture" and the beginning of a gauntlet-dropping challenge for all employees, not just the engineers, to aim high and to solve big problems.

One test for purpose-driven story statements is their usefulness in a crisis—if they are jettisoned at the first challenge, then, clearly, they were just empty words. But if they drive meaningful actions, then you know you've got something great, and this proved to be the case for NI when COVID-19 struck. Notes Sublett, "We have customers that we've been helping reimagine manufacturing lines, pivoting from one industry to making ventilators as an example, in a matter of days. We've been helping address this crisis, so it's not only inspiring to our employees, but also it's actually literally what we're doing."

COMMAND ALKON: TOGETHER WE BUILD AMAZING

When Ed Rusch arrived at Alabama-based Command Alkon in 2017 to take over the marketing reins, he found the company—which develops software for the construction industry—had been doing business essentially the same way for four decades. The sales team believed that direct contact was the only way to generate leads. The website was little more than a brochure with phone numbers. And, in truth, its construction-industry customers were still dependent on a lot of manual processes to connect supplier data with everyday jobs. Fortunately for Rusch, he had a mandate to help move the company and the industry into the digital age. But before he could do the big things, he needed to lay some important groundwork.

In our 2020 podcast interview, Rusch shared how he built "political capital" early in his tenure by implementing some quick fixes. Even though he knew there were huge improvement opportunities for the brand and big-picture messaging, he observes, "Why spend months figuring that out and not taking action on things that you can literally do within a couple hours?" Rusch advises, "I think as a general rule, keep it focused and keep it simple related to where you can find some wins quickly." Heeding his own good advice, Rusch added "Contact Us" forms and live chat to the website while training his team on how to interact with chat.

The results were nearly instantaneous. Explains Rusch, "Crazy enough, just within the first few hours of deploying some of those fundamental one-on-one type of capabilities, potential customers interacted with those digital channels. They reached out, drove leads, and within the first twenty-four hours, there were already qualified leads in the pipeline being handed over to sales." After a few more months of work, Rusch was able to create a demand-generating marketing program that paid for itself. This is how Rusch built the credibility he needed with the leadership team to tackle the bigger brand issues, including the development of a perfectly pithy story statement.

Rusch's process for repositioning Command Alkon began with a discovery phase in which he explored the attitude of Command Alkon's stakeholders toward the company. He first asked his peers, "If you had to describe what our company is in seven words or less or capture the essence of what our company is, what is that, and if you had to do it in less than thirty seconds, how would you respond?" From there, he says he "surveyed the workforce from the managerial leaders throughout the organization, all the way through to every role or function that wanted to participate. And then, most importantly, we went out and talked to our customers and had that same level of engagement with regards to how they understood us as a company." Working with an outside marketing agency, Rusch was able to crystallize the brand's new position in just four words: "Together We Build Amazing."

Looking at this language through multiple lenses should help you understand the power of perfecting pith. If you're an employee of Command Alkon, it is suddenly very easy for you to explain what your company does and feel pride in what you do. The word "together" speaks to the company's relatively new software platform that allows construction companies to work digitally with their suppliers. "We" addresses the need for and the power in teamwork. Of course, "build" covers the industry within which the company operates, and "amazing" sets a high-performance bar for everyone at the company.

Rusch breaks down the idea from a customer perspective starting with the first word: "The essence of that word was bringing 'together' all the people on a project so that they could do more together than they could on their own and the shared prosperity when they're working collaboratively with digital tools in order to do more with less." He adds, "The 'we' reinforces our partnership with our customers and the community and, more specifically, points to our collaboration platform and the technology products that underpinned the capability for people to actually do 'amazing' as a result of how we're acting on these projects in an orchestrated way." As I said, those are four hardworking words.

Importantly, Rusch understood that just the four words would not get the job done. He needed to make the idea real for employees, customers, and prospects. As such, he orchestrated a big kickoff party at a concert hall in Birmingham, which was streamed via a live telecast to their offices around the world. Toasting to "where we've been and where we're going as a team," Rusch also, "equipped everyone with pocket guides containing all the information about this new story so that they could go out and talk to the customers in the market with the type of confidence that we needed them to have." Adds Rusch, "Part of helping tell this story was actually going through and finding customer heroes and having our story really be a collection of their success stories, of how they've used technology and construction to transform their businesses." For prospects, Rusch developed a new website that reinforces the idea through videos, blog posts, and white papers.

PERFECTING PITHY PROCESS

Renegade's B2B brand strategy process offers a step-by-step guide for *perfecting pithy* and developing a compelling and transformative purpose-driven story statement. The process typically includes these four steps:

Discovery: We do a deep dive into the organization via interviews with employees, customers, and industry experts. This is also when we conduct our employee engagement research (see Chapter 7: Engage Employees First for a sample survey). At the end of this, we create a SWOT (strengths, weaknesses, opportunities, threats) document boiling all the information gathered down to a few core insights.

Strategic summary: Here, we define in the simplest terms "what" your brand does, "how" your brand does it, and "why" you do it. At the same time, and as referenced in Chapter 2, we'll go through the positioning exercise and identify your brand archetype (see Chapter 6). Sometimes, we'll create a Venn diagram that looks at the brand, the category, and the target's needs to see if there is a central notion that's ownable. The goal is to have the key elements of the brand strategy on one page, which supports the purpose-driven story statement.

Simplifying exercise: Here, we ask: What can we get rid of? For example, many B2B software companies create multiple subbrands and try to market them individually. Often, these names add little value to the sales or marketing process, and the whole company could benefit from offering one platform under one name with multiple modules. These modules can have clear descriptors but don't typically need their own brand name. Also, sometimes these modules can be combined to create more compelling and more distinctive offerings.

Purpose-driven story statement: This is where the pixie dust of what we do at Renegade comes in. It does take some creativity to put just the right words together in the right order. You will know you have a strong tagline when the language is inspiring, dramatic, distinctive, and functional (like explaining what category your company is in if it's not clear from the name) yet emotional. *And* it must be available. Always use the free Trademark Electronic Search System (TESS) offered by the US Patent and Trademark Office to see if anyone has used this same language. As a further precaution, do a Google search of the line both with and without quotation marks.

It doesn't hurt to have a long track record as a writer of these statements, so don't despair if your first attempts produce language that's been used before. It can take time, maybe even a career, to *perfect pithy*.

PERFECTING PITHY WITH PEDERSEN

Lindsey Pedersen, author of the book *Forging an Ironclad Brand: A Leader's Guide*, makes a powerful case for brand with a capital *B* while providing several useful tips on how to build one. Among these, she offers nine criteria for brand promises, which apply equally well to what we call purpose-driven story statements.

"For a brand to meet these criteria, leaders must make difficult choices and trade-offs," says Pedersen. "It can feel scary to decide so boldly and shine a spotlight on what you have selected. Yet choosing is what separates good leaders from great leaders, what separates flash-in-the-pan businesses from the ones that endure for generations." To wrap up this chapter, here are Pedersen's nine criteria along with real-world examples referenced in this book. Don't sweat it if you can't artfully craft a statement that meets all of these, but do go back to the drawing board if your tagline doesn't meet at least three.

1. *Big: Your brand promise must be big enough to matter.* This is the space you own in your customer's head. Make it a big space, a big promise.
   (Cofense, "Uniting Humanity Against Phishing" —chapter 4)

2. *Narrow: It must be narrow enough to own.* While your brand positioning must be big enough to matter, it also must be narrow enough for you to dominate. Choose a positioning you uniquely can own—one where you are not just better but also different.
   (Acoustic: "Marketing Technology Reimagined"—chapter 7)

3. *Asymmetrical: It must use your lopsided advantage.* Promise and deliver from your place of dramatically asymmetrical strength. It's asymmetrical because your edge comes not from being medium good at a lot of things but from being excellent at one thing.
   (Case Paper, "on the case"—chapter 5)

4. *Empathetic: It must address a deeply relevant and mean-ingful need.* Your positioning must genuinely have your customers' interests at heart.
    (Command Alkon, "Together We Build Amazing" —chapter 5)

5. *Optimally distinct: It must strike a balance between famil-iar and novel.* Familiarity gets you into the customer's mind, while novelty attracts the customer's attention.
    (SurveyMonkey, "Power the Curious"—chapter 5)

6. *Functional and emotional: It must be both practical and compelling to your customer.* Your offering must be at the critical intersection of your customer's heart and mind. If it's only emotional, they might not believe it. If it's only functional, they won't bond with it or be loyal to it.
    (*Family Circle*, "Where Family Comes First"—chapter 5)

7. *Sharp-edged: It must entail a single sharp-edged promise.* Your brand positioning must be simple and singular. It should be ridiculously clear to customers what you do and don't promise.
    (Utak, "Control Freaks"—chapter 3)

8. *Has teeth: It must be demonstrably true.* Your positioning must offer compelling, granular, concrete proof that it will deliver on its promise. It needs to be not only true but also demonstrably true.
    (NI, "Engineer Ambitiously"—chapter 5)

9. *Delivers: You must deliver on your brand promise across everything you do, from big to small, from new customer to loyal customer—consistently.* You don't just nail the letter of the promise but also the spirit of the promise.
    (Aetna, "You don't join us. We join you"—chapter 2)

KEY TAKEAWAYS

- If it takes more than eight words to tell your brand story, bring in an outside agency to help tighten it up.
- A purpose-driven story statement is more than a tagline; it compels a company to take actions that go well beyond the bounds of traditional marketing.
- For your story statement to take hold, it must be the result of a rigorous process that involves key organizational stakeholders.

CHAPTER 6

DELIGHT BY DESIGN

Summary: Aesthetics send signals. Kludgy design anywhere prevents brand love everywhere. Bake design into your organization.

Great brands, whether B2B or B2C, have a distinctive look, feel, and voice that you can recognize instantly. Think about Apple, Nike, and McDonald's. What comes to mind first? Probably their logos and then a particular aspect of their brand experience. Apple stores with their glass, wood, and T-shirted geniuses. The Nike swoosh and exerting athletes. The McDonald's arch, red french-fry holders, and clean bathrooms.

Now try to do this exercise for B2B brands. IBM is certainly top of mind with their slotted logo and the blue frames of their TV ads. But what else comes to mind? Beyond IBM's AI-showcase Watson that gained fame by competing against humans on *Jeopardy*, it's a bit of a blur, which is understandable given the size and complexity of their business. Even Salesforce, which enjoys near-universal awareness in the business world of the company name, has nowhere near the same level of understanding of its wide-ranging product offering. If you're a small- or medium-size business, you have an advantage. You can bake design into every aspect of your business, which will help you stand out rather easily from your kludgy competitors.

WHAT IS B2B BRAND DESIGN?

B2B brand design on its simplest level is the visual appearance of your brand, including logo, fonts, colors, and images. The more consistently these elements are used together, the more embedded they become in the minds of your target audiences. Done correctly, B2B brand design tells a story about your brand. Like a great picture, great design is worth a thousand, if not a million, words.

Let's start with color. To illustrate the power of color, let's look at the rental car industry. Which brand is gold? Red? Green? Easy, right? Hertz. Avis. National. Okay, now tell me what color is Budget, Dollar, and Alamo? That gets a lot harder. The consistent use of color can have a material impact on the way people think about your company. Gold is top-notch, classy. Red is strong, determined, and passionate. Green is associated with growth, safety, and money. This is an overly simplistic interpretation of the meaning of colors, but you can see how, in the world of rental car companies, color choices do have an impact on brand perceptions.

Here's a very easy exercise to see if your brand is using color to its advantage. Look at all the logos and visual design schemes of your competitive set. If you're creating a new category, then look at brands that are marketing to your same target audience. Evaluate each of the competitor's brand design just in terms of color. Is there one color or a combination of colors that they use consistently? Does this color convey something about the brand that distinguishes it from a sea of sameness?

In my 2020 interview with Carla Piñeyro Sublett, who was then leading a major rebranding initiative as CMO of National Instruments (now NI), Sublett noted, "Color was probably the most difficult and most controversial change. If anything, I would say, of the eleven-month process, we were slowed by about forty-five days on the debate of color alone." She adds, "The funny thing is, when we set out to do the work, we did a wall test to compare competitors' brand colors, and what we learned in that wall test is that everybody in our space, with the exception of one, were blue." Ultimately, NI shifted to a "very vibrant green," giving a new, action-oriented vibe to the forty-year-old brand.

HOW TO USE COLOR FOR B2B BRANDING

Imagine you're an accountant. Or a bookkeeper. Is it that hard? Work with me here. Let's just say you're walking through a busy trade show for business professionals with about thirty exhibitors. Twenty-nine of the booths use muted colors. One of them uses orange. And not just in their signage and logo. Every one of the twenty-five or so staffers at this booth is wearing an orange T-shirt. Bright orange. And they have smiles on their faces. And this rather large booth is packed with visitors. It calls to them. It calls to you. Irresistibly. Like moths to a flame. But no one is getting burned except for the other exhibitors.

This is a true story that I witnessed. I just can't name the brand. What I can tell you is that the orange brand enjoyed three times the traffic of the other less colorful exhibitors. Crowds attract crowds. So do compelling offers coupled with an unexpected color. As such, the orange booth stayed busy the whole day while the others were practically empty. This is what it means to cut through.

When ProsperWorks decided to rebrand, it changed its name to Copper in late 2018 and made the audacious choice of pink for all its branding. For a software company targeting other businesses, this was a bold move. It also reflected a dramatic transformation of their product, which the company redesigned from the ground up. How better to signal a major change than using an unexpected color? Here's how Morgan Norman, then the CMO of Copper, explains their choice of pink in our podcast interview "Copper, Blue + Pink: An Artful Name Change":

> If you line up company logos by color, sadly, under blue, you're going to see everyone. Everyone uses the lovely world of blues in enterprise software. And when we looked at all this, we saw an opportunity. The area where it was wide open was pink. No one had done it.

It's gutsy. It's modern. It's fresh. It's different. It brings a
different air to things, a different expression to things,
I think some people really absolutely love it, and some
people are like "wow that's intense." But that actually
was the goal. The goal was to be something radically
different that you wouldn't see in CRM.

Color is but one aspect of brand design. As mentioned earlier,
type, visuals, and even language can have a huge impact on B2B brand
design. One way to assess your organization's appreciation for brand
design is to find out when the first in-house designer was hired. If
that hire happened early on, no doubt you'll see design permeate the
organization, not just from an identity standpoint but also from a user
experience perspective. Way back in 2010, Scott Harrison, founder of
Charity Water, told me for a FastCompany.com story called "Who the
Heck Are the Bayaka and 7 Other Questions for Aspiring Leaders": "To
solve a problem as big as the water crisis, we would need to create an
epic brand." And to do that, Harrison's second hire was an art director/
videographer. To this day, Charity Water is the rare nonprofit with a
truly enviable brand, all designed on a shoestring.

You may not always notice good or great design, but you'll probably
notice when it is absent. Think about a recent website visit. Did you
find what you were looking for in a matter of seconds? Did the landing
page calm you or make you anxious? Was the design consistent? Great
designers solve problems. Bad design creates them.

A QUICK LOOK AT LOGO DESIGN

Logos are another design area in which entire books have been written, so this section is meant just to call your attention to the basics.
The first rule of logo design is to work with experts. These talented
individuals have a vocabulary unto themselves and can ascribe meaning to every curve of every font and every edge of every symbol. They
can tell you when the tension between your name and your symbol
(the mark next to your name—think Nike's swoosh) is a good thing
and when they are fighting each other for attention. Don't be tempted

by online offers to design your logo for a few hundred dollars: given the importance of your logo (name and mark) to every aspect of your business and how long a good logo will last, you'll want to think twice before skimping on design fees.

The next rule is: don't waste time and money redesigning your logo unless this change coincides with and can reinforce a substantial change for your product or service. You can repaint a broken-down car, but that won't fool the driver or keep it out of the shop. Conversely, if you have made substantive changes to your product or service, perhaps setting your brand up to enter new markets, then consider deploying a new logo to help signal this big change to the marketplace, especially if the previous logo had design flaws.

Design flaws may seem like a subjective topic, but allow me to suggest a few that aren't:

- The logo is only legible at large sizes, making it unusable online or on business cards
- The logo is so wide that when it is shown with other logos, it is the least visible
- The logo looks like another better-known brand
- The symbol accompanying your name is distracting, irrelevant, or so intricate that it creates production challenges
- When you compare your logo with the others in your category, yours blends in

The most common time to change your logo is when you also change your name. This was the case for TRUSTe when it changed its corporate name to TrustArc in 2017. In our 2019 podcast interview, CMO Dave Deasy explained first the need for the name change: "It was difficult to convince a lot of companies that we were a technology company, because when they would hear the TRUSTe name, they would immediately think to themselves that we were just the certification company."

Given the business need to change its name, the development of a new logo also created an opportunity for an evolved brand personality. As Deasy explains, "It wasn't as much trying to run away from our image as it was leveraging the good parts while changing enough to help create a new identity." And here's the most instructive part for you creative-leaning marketers: Deasy challenged his logo design agency to "just get crazy and see if there's something that you can do with animals." Animals?

Okay, the point here isn't to ask your agency to incorporate animals into your new logo. The point is just to inspire them, to challenge them to explore different avenues. This is what cool CATS do! Deasy thought of animals because he'd noticed other companies using them. This led to the incorporation of a finlike notch in the arc above the TrustArc logo. And that, in turn, led the brand to dolphins. Yup, dolphins. Here's *that* story from Deasy:

> But why dolphins? And our design firm came back with a story about how the dolphin fit with the arc, starting with a lot of symbolism around the idea. Dolphins are very intelligent. They're also very friendly. And in general, people like dolphins. At the same time, they're actually very fierce animals. So pretty quickly, they sold us on this notion of the arcs with a little bump on them, which became this idea of the dolphins. And while there's nothing to do between dolphins and privacy, all of a sudden, it started to tie our new identity together in a nice way.

To put a bow on this story, dolphins played an important role in the launch of TrustArc, which I should remind you is in the serious space of internet privacy. Initially just planned as a gift for employees, little plush dolphins became the coveted giveaway at TrustArc launch parties and subsequent trade shows. This surprised Deasy, since "we sell to lawyers, people with legal backgrounds and complaints backgrounds." As it turns out, these people are humans too, with an apparently strong attraction to dolphins. Even in logo design, it pays to be a renegade marketer.

As an artful CMO, you need not limit your delightful design to things you can visualize. For example, another area that can be designed to deliver distinctive results is brand voice, so let's turn our attention to that area now.

BRAND VOICE DESIGN

Great brands have a consistent personality, speaking to us in the same appealing tone and manner no matter where you encounter them. This personality is often summed up by what our industry calls "brand voice." A well-defined brand voice has many advantages to the marketer and the company. Understanding how the brand speaks and how it doesn't means that no matter where a customer or prospect encounters the brand, the voice—and by extension, the experience—will be consistent. It also means that your ever-growing team of content creators won't issue materials that are "off brand."

Which begs the question, how do you determine your brand voice? For smaller companies, the brand voice often stems from the unique character of the founder. I've already mentioned how Ben Cohen and Jerry Greenfield imbued their company with fun from the start, making sure they never took anything too seriously other than the creation of deliciously playful ice-cream experiences. You can still hear Steve Jobs's voice in the original version of Apple's famous "Think Different" campaign and even though Richard Dreyfuss narrated the ads that aired on TV, his reading clearly echoes Jobs's version. And more to the point, Jobs's distinct sensibility continues to inform just about every aspect of Apple's brand. But what of companies with more reticent founders?

One approach that we find extremely useful for identifying a distinctive brand voice is the use of archetypes. Developed by Carl Jung and since refined by his adherents, there are twelve Jungian archetypes to choose from. These archetypes like Joker (think Geico, Bud Light) and Explorer (think Jeep, Patagonia), have rich backstories that can help inform, distinguish, and hold together all of your marketing activities. PsychologistWorld.com has a free Jungian Archetype Test to help you assess the archetype with which your brand currently best aligns. By the way, taking the test is a bit tricky in that you have to imagine you're answering as if you were the brand. You may need to have a couple of individuals with a deep understanding of your company take the test to get conclusive results.

Some companies try this as a leadership team exercise. The challenge with this approach is that many executives want to see their brand as the hero, the brand that saves the day. And Hero is indeed an archetype that works for some brands like Nike, FedEx, and the United States Marine Corps. But Hero is problematic for many B2B brands, especially software providers, since many of them are enablers of their customers' heroics. They are Merlin to young Arthur, Obi-Wan Kenobi to Luke Skywalker. This, in turn, leads many B2B brands to think of themselves as the Sage, or wise advisor (like IBM, Google, *The Economist*).

Finding the right archetype for your brand is not just a question of how you've spoken in the past or how you see yourself talking in the future. It's also important to consider your larger competitors, assuming any of them have established a clear and consistent voice in the marketplace. If every one of your competitors is presenting themselves as the wise Sage, it's obvious that adopting that same voice won't help you cut through. On the other hand, very few brands in any industry, especially in the business-to-business arena, have the bravery to be the Joker brand. That takes courage and artfulness, since humor is often in the eye of the beholder.

But choosing an unlikely archetype in your category can be hugely effective. It's simply a case of zigging when others zag. It's worth noting here that one brand that did have the courage to adopt the Joker archetype is Case Paper, a "case" shared in detail in Chapter 5. As you learned, Case Paper had a long history of using humor dating back to the 1960s. Sometimes your brand voice is already lurking in your archives, or, as you'll see in the next case, sometimes you need to enlist others to help you express it in the most compelling way possible.

DESIGNING YOUR BRAND VOICE THROUGH OTHERS

In 2017, Toni Clayton-Hine, then Xerox SVP and chief marketing officer, was looking for a dramatic way to get businesses to rethink their perceptions of the company. This was not an easy task, given the company's history. After all, Xerox is to copying as FedEx is to shipping. Both are synonymous with their category. Their names have even become verbs. Under most circumstances, this is the pinnacle of branding, but for Xerox, which wanted to evolve past its roots in the copier business, this category association was problematic. Somehow, Xerox needed to break away from its heritage.

To tell a fresh story about Xerox, Clayton-Hine assembled fourteen of the world's greatest storytellers and didn't ask them to write about Xerox. Instead, they were simply asked to voice their thoughts about the modern workplace. Explains Clayton-Hine, "We literally asked them, with no boundaries, to contribute their perspectives on the modern workplace. So, Lee Child, Aimee Mann, Jonathan Coulter, Roxane Gay, and more were all able to contribute some form of writing—a song, an essay, fiction—in their own style. We got to see these different elements of what they consider work, and what we quickly saw is that work is definitely not a place anymore. All of these guys came together, contributing their chapters."

Sloane Crosley, a *New York Times* bestselling essayist, created "the connective tissue between these works to help formulate an ebook called *Set the Page Free*," Clayton-Hine says. In a sense, multiple voices become one. This program also featured videos with the authors as well as live events at the 92nd Street Y in New York City. Clayton-Hine summarized the program's success in our 2018 interview: "From there, we could tell the story of how this interesting project came together, and we could leverage the celebrity of the authors and organizations involved. All of that helped our marketing and amplified the message. We got a lot of PR amplification simply because it was, as we had hoped, an interesting 'story.'"

We've covered a lot of territory in this chapter but by no means have done justice to the entire world of design and its critical importance to marketing success. For logo design, I highly recommend reading *Logo Design Love: A Guide to Creating Iconic Brand Identities* by David Airey or *Designing Brand Identity: An Essential Guide for the Whole Branding Team* by Alina Wheeler.

KEY TAKEAWAYS

- Finding your unique combination of brand color and brand voice will clearly differentiate your brand.
- If your logo and design elements feature the same color as key competitors, it's time to revisit your design schema.
- If you speak in the same voice as your key competitors, it's time to revisit your brand archetype.

PART III

THOUGHTFUL EXECUTION

Well done is better than well said.
—Benjamin Franklin

A marketer's *thoughtful execution* is simply about doing stuff—thoughtful stuff for your employees, customers, prospects, and all your other audiences. Doing comes in many forms (entertain, educate, inspire, enlighten) but is most noteworthy for what it isn't: feature-driven messaging about your product or service. It starts from a place of respect: that you need to earn the right to someone's time. It reflects the arrival of what I call the "give-to-get economy" in which we marketers need to give something of value in order to get something in return, typically time and attention.

Thoughtful execution is the polar opposite of feature-driven advertising, the kind that hopes to annoy or bludgeon you into action. And while that more traditional approach still has its advocates and still works for many, few B2B brands have a large-enough budget or a short-enough sales cycle to take this route. The alternative is to build your brand by doing stuff that makes it easier for your employees to evangelize, your customers to be advocates, and your prospects to feel good about adding you to their short list.

In this section, we'll walk you through why employees should be your first target yet are often the most overlooked and underutilized source of brand evangelism. For that, you'll be introduced to CMOs who have become masters at marketing to employees (Chapter 7: Engage Employees First). We'll then move on to your customers and why they need to be an important part of any new marketing or branding initiative (Chapter 8: Cultivate Customer Champions). And finally, we'll share how you can *sell through service*, an approach that gained even more traction when the pandemic took in-person events off the options list (Chapter 9: Sell through Service).

CHAPTER 7

ENGAGE EMPLOYEES FIRST

Summary: If employees don't believe, no one will. They are the front line that drives the bottom line. When they're inspired, goodness follows.

In Chapter 4, we discussed the importance of involving your whole organization in the strategic development process. As part of this, we recommended fielding an employee survey at the start of your marketing journey. Not only will this research provide useful benchmarks to track against after your new program is in the marketplace, but it may also yield valuable insights that can drive your efforts.

In an employee survey that Renegade fielded in 2019 for one of our clients, we uncovered a couple of lingering issues from a previous rebranding effort. As such, when we developed the new plan, we were able to include specific components that addressed past issues and ensured that the new program would be well received. Here's the key— if employees don't believe in the brand, if they can't embody the spirit of the brand, then there is little hope that your marketing activities will make a difference. Therefore, for every B2B marketing or rebranding program, we recommend that employee communications happen in advance of any external activities.

The importance of internal communications is not a debate. In our proprietary research study among B2B CMOs in 2019 and 2020, more than 90 percent acknowledged the critical importance of employee communications. But, and there's a great big *but* here, two-thirds of these same CMOs allowed less than one month of internal comms before launching externally. This inconsistency is significant. Basically, these CMOs are saying, "Our new marketing initiative does not require any substantive organizational changes or meaningful educational efforts." What's wrong with this picture? A lot.

Becoming a renegade marketer is about more than crafting words, logos, and pictures. It starts by making a distinctive promise to the marketplace and then delivering on that promise in as many ways as possible and as consistently as possible. At the center of this promise are your employees. *Employees make your promise real.* And if you're making a new promise, there's a pretty good chance you're going to need to make some changes to how you do business, how you interact with your customers, and how you recruit new employees. All these things need to be aligned.

ACOUSTIC: THE BILLION-DOLLAR START-UP

In July 2019, the marketing technology division within IBM spun out into a brand-new company soon to be called Acoustic. Suddenly more than a thousand employees servicing more than thirty-five hundred customers in twenty-one countries had to disassociate from the well-known IBM Watson brand and start again. For Norman Guadagno, the CMO who arrived two months later, this was to be an epic challenge, not just building a brand but also building a marketing organization while helping to build a company. (It's a good thing Guadagno is a builder, having helped Carbonite more than double during his CMO tenure from 2016 to 2019.)

But where to start? For Guadagno, whose first day coincided with the new HR chief's arrival, the answer may surprise you. Reports Guadagno, "Building a brand starts on day one with an employee. In fact, it starts before day one when first-time prospective employees find out about a company and they're recruited." Partnering with HR, they focused on defining the vision, mission, and values for Acoustic and then establishing a cadence for communicating the new direction to the company. With this foundation in place, it was time to tackle positioning.

For Guadagno, the big insight sprang from the realization that most of his larger competitors, and the company they spun out of, were trying to solve a myriad of problems for a broad range of target audiences. Not Acoustic. Explains Guadagno, "We're a thousand people just focused on this set of marketing technology, on campaign automation, on experience analytics, journey analytics, personalization, content management. We're not trying to do everything. We're not trying to be a back office, solve every IT problem for a company. We're trying to solve problems for the marketers from marketing."

Now armed with the brand promise of "marketing technology reimagined," and ready for a big launch campaign in March 2020, Guadagno, along with the rest of the world, was sideswiped by the pandemic. Already used to working remotely (Acoustic was headquartered in New York, and Guadagno lives in Boston), the real challenge was trying to sustain "that human connection of live people, one to one." To address that, Guadagno and the head of HR began cohosting One Acoustic Live—companywide virtual gatherings at which "we bring topics up and have dialogues so that we can get the most out of people being online around the world." While many companies turned to virtual "town halls" during the pandemic, it is unusual that these are led by the CMO in partnership with HR, and reflects the importance to the overall effectiveness of Acoustic marketing that Guadagno bestows upon employee engagement.

Ran Gishri, CMO at Taboola, a fast-growing advertising technology company, sees "an interesting trend in the coming together of marketing and HR as more and more companies realize that hiring and retaining employees is fairly similar to acquiring and retaining customers; hence, the same methodologies and skills apply." Recognizing this, Gishri notes that "at Taboola, employer branding is under brand marketing; that team has been working very closely with HR and already made a huge impact on our hiring in a highly competitive environment."

To bang this drum a bit louder: having new positioning is essentially useless unless it is fully embraced and operationalized by your entire organization. With your newfound courage and artful tact, no doubt you're ready to bring your company to the promised land of your new promise. When employees fully understand the significance of what you, the marketer, are doing and believe they are part of something bigger than themselves, the results are often seismic. That's why the cool CATS of marketing make employee engagement a top priority.

TAKING EMPLOYEES BACK TO SCHOOL

Now, what happens if your employees are your product? How do you make sure that the experience that one customer has with one employee is the same as a different customer might have with a different employee? Now imagine you have more than four hundred thousand employees in more than a hundred countries around the world. That's exactly the situation Deloitte faces with their consulting practice, and how they approach this challenge is quite interesting.

Meet Diana O'Brien, a twenty-five-year veteran at Deloitte and their global CMO from March 2015 to August 2020. When I interviewed O'Brien in late 2018, we discussed her prior role and perhaps proudest accomplishment—starting Deloitte University. Featuring a massive training facility, including hotel rooms and a conference center at which every employee receives skills training on things like listening, empathy, leadership, and storytelling, this university teaches all the skills that it takes to be not just a successful consultant but a beloved "Deloitter." Talk about engaging employees first in a highly thoughtful manner!

Growing a community of leaders is an important goal for many companies, but not typically one that is undertaken during a recession with a $300 million investment in a facility stretching over a hundred acres. Deloitte's CEO back in 2011, Joe Echevarria, had the foresight to make this commitment and the smarts to put Diana O'Brien in charge of it, even though she was a bit skeptical at first. Reassured by Echevarria, O'Brien spearheaded this remarkable program that now trains sixty-five thousand employees every year, uniting them with a common culture and shared understanding of what makes an effective consultant.

In our conversation, O'Brien, who was recognized by *Forbes* as one of the World's Most Influential CMOs for several years running, shared how Deloitte University is the cornerstone to building a strong and consistent employee culture. First off, it's the recognition "that Deloitte University is more than a place; it's a mindset. It's that you carry with you everywhere you're a leader, and at any moment you could be asked to lead, and that's leading a team meeting that could be leading a client conversation. It's that we're leaders and we need to be prepared to do that. And so culturally, it is the soul of our firm."

The sequence of curriculum is also worth highlighting. It starts with the "art of empathy," then moves to the "art of the story," followed by the "art of inquiry." About empathy, O'Brien insists it can be taught, "particularly by helping people understand differences and how to help people feel that they belong." Digging deeper, this curriculum helps Deloitters understand the need to express empathy differently to four identified personality types: drivers, integrators, pioneers, and guardians. Explains O'Brien, "We help people to understand and think through what it means to think and walk in someone else's shoes." For Deloitte, the art of empathy is a foundational attribute for a consulting company. Empathy helps employees communicate better internally. It is also vital when interacting with clients.

The art of storytelling is also important at Deloitte. Employees are taught how to connect their story or stories to a client as well as the company. Stories are meant to inspire and spark action. Stories allow employees to connect the personal to why they do what they do. Armed with empathy and the ability to tell stories, Deloitters are better and more consistent communicators.

Deloitte's story?

Deloitte chooses to heavily invest in its employees because, in truth, employees are the brand. Clients don't work with Deloitte, they work with "Deloitters." And with more than four hundred thousand Deloitters posted around the world, having a shared understanding of the brand and its value is not a luxury, it is a necessity. To deliver on its promise of "making an impact that matters," Deloitte must first make an impact that matters on its number-one success determinant—employees.

In O'Brien's own words: "Do they feel like they are in an environment that we want them to create for our clients? If employees don't feel that they can speak up or bring their authentic selves, if they don't feel that they are being shown empathy, or given the right tools, then they're not going to show up that way for our clients."

Even in her roles as US CMO, which she assumed in 2014, and global CMO, which was added in 2018, O'Brien continued to invest heavily in culture-building activities, spending more than 50 percent of her time out in the field doing just that. In the pantheon of such ageless truisms as "diligence is the mother of good luck" and "force sits upon reason's back," we cool CATS can now add, with O'Brien's inspiration, "branding begins at home."

EMPLOYEE ENGAGEMENT IN A PANDEMIC

Prior to the pandemic, Jeff Perkins, CMO of ParkMobile, was already a believer in the importance of employee engagement. When he arrived at the company in 2016, he helped lead a reassessment of the company's mission and vision along with "a core value workshop for the executive team." These values are: "a healthy obsession with customer experience, act with integrity, sweat the small stuff, play well with others, rise and fall together, and support our people, support our community." Communicating these values became an ongoing obsession for Perkins, including the creation of the annual Core Value Awards, which "recognize the people who embody our six core values." But he didn't stop there.

Perkins personally drafted a weekly employee newsletter for six months with touches of humor highlighting "things happening across the company that everybody should be excited about." He felt he needed to be the author, at least at first, because he "had more of an executive view of the company, and I could put together the right content, the things that were impacting the business." Perkins also instituted bimonthly all-hands lunches for sharing and learning, weekly companywide happy hours, and quarterly Innovation Weeks. This last program involved a *Shark Tank*–like competition complete with idea pitches from cross-disciplined teams and a judging panel. Prizes were awarded to the winning team, although the real benefit was that employees got a little breathing room from the daily grind "to go and explore, to experiment, to try out some new toys or some new tech tools," recalled Perkins just two months before the pandemic.

Perkins and I spoke several times after COVID-19-related shutdowns hit ParkMobile's business particularly hard. Keep in mind, there were several months in 2020 during which commuters stopped driving into cities altogether. No drivers. No parking. No business for ParkMobile's parking app. But there was a bit of light in the darkness. Their app made for touchless metering, and suddenly, cities that had been slow to adopt this new tech embraced it with unprecedented speed. And because of all the goodwill built among their employees, the transition to working from home was relatively smooth and employee morale remained high. As it turns out, engaging employees first is not just a critical priority for marketing success; it also acts as an insurance policy in the event of an unexpected crisis.

ENGAGING EMPLOYEES FIRST INCLUDES MEASUREMENT

At the start of any brand strategy engagement, we always encourage CMOs to field an employee study. These studies are critical for many reasons. First, they send a clear signal to employees that the company leadership cares about their opinions. Second, they provide a benchmark for employee attitudes about the brand by which you can track progress over time. Third, these studies can inform the brand story, assuming you ask the right questions. And fourth, they can inform your internal communications plan and the degree to which you need to transform internal perceptions about the brand. Getting so much out of one survey is the hallmark of a true renegade marketer!

At a minimum, we recommend an annual employee satisfaction (e-sat) survey that gauges how your employees feel about the company, its purpose, its products, its service, its marketing, and the management. You can also include open-ended questions that will help you assess the culture, identify any lingering issues, and often uncover new opportunities. This type of survey is easy to field (we tend to use SurveyMonkey) and can provide invaluable insights in two weeks or less. Aim for between 33 to 50 percent participation, depending on your company's size, and you may need to send a few emails to remind employees of this opportunity to provide important feedback.

SAMPLE EMPLOYEE SURVEY

1. Please identify the office you work from mainly. (from drop-down menu)
2. Please identify your department. (from drop-down menu)
3. How many years have you been with Company X? (less than a year, one to two years, three to four years, more than five years)
4. It is easy for me to explain what Company X does to others outside the company.
5. The leaders at Company X have communicated a vision that motivates me.
6. The leaders at Company X keep staff informed about what is happening.
7. I am proud to tell people that I work for Company X.
8. Company X motivates me to go beyond what I would do in a similar role elsewhere.
9. I am inspired to meet my goals at work.
10. I am proud of the marketing we do for the Company X brand.
11. Company X has a clearly defined purpose. (yes/no)
12. If yes, please describe Company X's purpose. (open-ended)
13. How likely are you to recommend Company X as a great place to work to a friend? (scale zero to ten)
14. What four words would you use to describe the culture at Company X? (four empty slots)
15. What do you like best about working at Company X? (open-ended)

16. What do you think are the company's greatest strengths? (open-ended)
17. What's the one thing you'd like Company X to improve upon? (open-ended)
18. Is there something else you think we should have asked you in this survey? (open-ended)

Questions four to ten use the following options as answers:

- Strongly disagree
- Disagree
- Neutral/Neither agree nor disagree
- Agree
- Strongly agree

WHAT TO LOOK FOR IN EMPLOYEE SURVEYS

The first time you field an employee survey, think of it mainly as a benchmark from which to consider actions and measure future improvements. Look at the ratings in questions four to ten relative to each other. If you see one really low score and one really high one, then it is worth examining each more closely. If they're all in the same range, then just consider these as base-level scores to compare against after you've implemented substantial changes.

If as a company you've already invested in NPS (net promoter score) to measure customer satisfaction, then you may want to pay particular attention to question thirteen, which is known as eNPS (employee net promoter score). To calculate eNPS, you need to subtract the percentage of "detractors" (employees who rate the company at zero through six) from the percentage of "promoters" (those who rate the company at nine or ten), thus yielding a net score. The average eNPS is between 15 and 20, depending on whose research you want to believe. If your score ends up being below this, then look at it as both an opportunity for improvement and a defense for spending more energy on employee engagement programs.

Questions one to three will allow you to sort the data by office, by department, and by longevity. Sometimes this will yield helpful insights, like a morale issue in a particular office or department. This information will help you target your internal programs.

Ran Avrahamy, CMO of AppsFlyer, is a big fan of keeping employee studies and metrics simple: "For AppsFlyer employees, our main metric is pride. Being proud is a notion that transcends way above being happy with your work environment and salary. It is about identifying with the company values and goals, feeling satisfied with what you do, and feeling love and respect for your colleagues. It is extremely valuable."

ENGAGED EMPLOYEES LOWER COSTS

Another critical reason to *engage employees first* is that engaged employees, especially ones who unite behind your brand purpose, are consistently more productive and more likely to stay longer, which, in turn, lowers recruiting and training expenses. Engaged employees are also far more likely to say positive things about your company to their friends and on all-important employer review sites like Glassdoor—with the result that your recruiting costs will also go down since your recruiting yield will go up. When this happens, you have what some call a healthy "employer brand." Measuring the health of your employer brand can thus include e-sat, as we've discussed already, and recruiting yield—also known as "new employee conversion rate"—which is as simple as dividing the total number of offers extended by the offers accepted. (Note: you'll see these two metrics again in Chapter 10.)

MORE ENGAGEMENT IDEAS

In sum, engaging employees is not an optional luxury for renegade marketers. It's a necessity, and it warrants tracking. As you've seen in this chapter, there are myriad ways of engaging employees. Here are a few examples that Renegade clients and others have adapted to align with their new brand stories:

- Start an employee book club in which everyone reads the same book each month.
- Develop a proprietary training program that reinforces your new brand promise.
- Revise the employee evaluation form to emphasize updated brand promise.
- Develop an awards program that brings the new promise to life.
- Establish a reverse mentoring program such that execs are teaching leadership to entry-level employees, who, in turn, share insights about their generation and/or social media know-how.
- Create a mobile app that enables employees to recognize other employees.
- Deploy an employee social media ambassador program.
- Train employees on how to build their personal brands in alignment with the company brand.
- Create special days or weeks for coming up with new ideas.

KEY TAKEAWAYS

- Renegade marketers never bypass employees at any stage of their efforts.
- Before launching a new campaign, allow sufficient time for employee education—if they don't embrace it, no one will!
- Engaging employees is a never-ending process.

CHAPTER 8

CULTIVATE CUSTOMER CHAMPIONS

Summary: Do what it takes to engender brand love. Make the customers the heroes of your story. Inspire them to share the wonders of your product/service.

It seems obvious enough. Every B2B company is in the business of acquiring new customers while keeping current ones for as long as possible. And typically, the business priorities are written in exactly that order. In this book, we recommend switching the order and focusing on your current customers before prospects. After engaging employees, *cultivating customer champions* needs to be the top organizational priority, especially when embarking on a rebranding effort. Wait, what?

Let's step back for a second. You're the CMO. You've gone through a B2B rebranding process. You've found your unique positioning informed by purpose and have cleverly expressed it in eight words or less. You've introduced the idea to employees and even retrained them to deliver upon the new promise. So far, so good. Now, why not just take this directly to your prospects and see the new revenue begin to flow? Simple. If your customers can't see their way to embracing your new brand story, chances are it will die before its time, never turning into the prospect-attracting nectar you so covet.

There are several reasons for this. First, almost no B2B transactions occur without a reference check in one form or another. In fact, few of us even take a meeting without first googling that individual and the company for which they work. Inevitably, we'll find ourselves looking at online reviews and making snap rejections. Who wants to waste time meeting with a company that has a poor reputation?

A second reason is that few prospective customers are daring enough to "eat the first oyster," so to speak. Much to the frustration of many sales reps, one of the first questions a potential B2B customer will ask is: "Have you worked with a company like mine?" They are simply seeking reassurances that your product or service will work for them, that you understand the challenges of their industry and have already solved them. It's not an unreasonable question, even if it does demonstrate a certain lack of imagination.

The third reason to *cultivate customer champions* when embarking on a new marketing program is that you really need customer buy-in. Assuming your new campaign is more than a fresh coat of paint on an old barn—one that encompasses meaningful changes to your customer experience, if not the product itself—then you'll want your customers on board from the earliest possible stages. Ideally, your top customers are brought in during the development phase to help inform if not validate your new direction.

The fourth and most recent reason for *cultivating customer champions* is that these folks could end up being your key to surviving the next downturn. They certainly were the reason that many B2B brands weathered 2020 in better shape than they were anticipating when the pandemic-related lockdown started in March. Let's take a modest detour to talk about what happened in mid-2020 and the long-term lessons learned.

MAKING YOUR BRAND ESSENTIAL

In the early days of the pandemic-induced lockdown, several cloud-based B2B brands saw their businesses skyrocket (e.g., Zoom, Slack,

Talkdesk). The reason: they played some role in helping other businesses make the transition from an office-based staff to working from home. Everything needed to move to the cloud, from communications to customer support to security to collaboration to accounting to you name it. As one pundit put it, six years of digital transformation were compressed into six months. What was once considered a "nice to have" option was suddenly an essential need. "Essential" being the operative word. Which was great for those "right place, right time" brands. And for everyone else, they faced a daunting new challenge.

Around May 2020, CFOs became what I dubbed "CF Nos." In the face of enormous uncertainty and a desire to preserve capital, these typically cautious individuals suddenly put the kibosh on any pending deal that wasn't deemed essential. If your product or service couldn't meet the "essential" smell test or couldn't demonstrate an extraordinarily fast return on investment, then you were told to come back in 2021! This concept is called "speed to value," and it's one that still haunts many enterprise software salespeople who know their brand's payback often takes many months, if not years.

It's fair to ask at this point, "Hey, Drew, what does all of this have to do with *cultivating customer champions*?" I'm getting there, I promise. Staring at a dramatic decrease in lead flow and an extension in how long it took to close leads, several savvy marketers recognized that their best hope of surviving the slowdown was securing their current customers. This meant marketing and the rest of the organization had to take off their sales hats and embrace a new kind of customer centricity. One CMO I know was part of an executive team that contacted every single customer right as the pandemic began, checking in on the health of each business and in some cases offering extended payment terms. It wasn't entirely altruistic—in exchange for delayed payments, they gained longer contract terms and, in some cases, a newfound willingness to provide testimonials and case histories.

Other CMOs I spoke with during the peak of the crisis noted that going back to their customers to "check in on them" was more than just a survival strategy. It turned out to be a business driver, especially for those who had software or services that the customer wasn't aware of or could prove to be of benefit during the pandemic. In crass terms, this type of approach is called "cross-selling" and "upselling." But in

2020, it was anything but crass. It was good business. It was smart business. It was business at a moment when many others saw none.

At some point, the pandemic will be a memory many will have happily forgotten. But not renegade marketers. The importance of generating brand love, of taking care of your customers during good times and bad, should never be forgotten. As is the need to always think about how your business can be considered "essential" to both customers and prospects. Given the importance of having strong customer relationships, it is little wonder that many CMOs are now assuming or seeking responsibility for customer success. This is also why we'll spend some time together on the basics of *cultivating customer champions.*

BEFORE THEY CAN BE CHAMPIONS, THEY MUST BE SATISFIED

Let's start with the basics. Your product or service comes with a fundamental promise in terms of performance. Expectations are set during the sales and procurement process. At a minimum, these expectations must be met. No duh, right? But before breezing by this Business 101 observation, are you absolutely sure your product or service is meeting expectations? One way to know is to read online reviews. Another is to talk to your customers regularly about your performance. A third is to measure customer satisfaction (c-sat) at regular intervals, the most common measure today being net promoter score (NPS).

Fred Reichheld's seminal book, *The Ultimate Question*, launched an entire industry around a single question to measure c-sat. Though some of Reichheld's early data has subsequently been disputed, NPS remains a stalwart of measuring customer satisfaction, via an easy question to ask: on a scale of zero to ten, zero being the lowest and ten being the highest, how likely are you to recommend XYZ product/ service to a friend or associate? (We met NPS's sibling eNPS in Chapter 4.) While we'll explore alternative measures in Chapter 10, the point here is that you recognize the need to meet, if not exceed, customer expectations and are committed to some form of measuring this.

HOW CAN YOU CULTIVATE B2B CUSTOMERS?

Beyond the basics, there are various ways for renegade marketers to cultivate customers. Of course, some of the options depend on your category or industry and the standards that have been set. If, for example, everyone in your software segment offers twenty-four-seven live customer support, then not offering it may distinguish your brand in a bad way.

There may also be basic product-level functionality that needs to be factored in. We were doing some customer interviews for one of our clients when we learned that their c-sat was higher for customers who had purchased the analytics module on top of the basic product. This analytics module enabled customers to see the impact of the software and thus made them feel better about the overall return on investment. Maybe you have a similarly tiered offering. As a result, you may be charging your customers extra for something that affects their likelihood of recommending your brand. If so, maybe it's time to bake that into your basic product offering, even if it means charging more.

Assuming your product or service meets—or better yet, exceeds—performance expectations, then we can move on to the various ways to *cultivate customer champions.* Here are some suggestions:

Customer Advisory Boards. One good place to start is with customer advisory boards, or CABs. CABs are quite common among SaaS (software as a service) brands that target enterprises and are usually made up of ten to twenty highly engaged customers, the ones who consistently serve as references and feel a proprietary relationship with the brand. It's easy to rationalize giving these folks a special level of treatment—they are, in fact, the crown jewel of your company—so it is worth spending a bit more time on building out your customer advisory board.

When setting up CABs, it is important to determine what's in it for your customer. Some will appreciate the chance to have a voice about future iterations of your product, which is usually a reflection of how important your product is to their success. Some will welcome the recognition, especially if you feature them in flattering video case histories that they can use in their own marketing. Some will like the opportunity to network with their peers, which CAB meetings can provide. Still others may feel the need for more material compensation like a product discount and/or credits that can be applied to paid training modules. Which brings us to customer reward programs.

Loyalty Programs. Over the last four decades, airlines and credit card companies, among others, have trained most of us to enroll in points-based loyalty programs. The structures are typically quite simple: the more you spend, the more rewards you earn. Lately, many B2B brands are adopting their own variants of this model. The only twist is that reward points can be earned through several actions and redeemed in different ways. These actions include spending more, participating in proof-of-performance pilots for new products, providing referrals, being a reference, and starring in video testimonials or case histories. Redemption options go well beyond product discounts to earning points for training, conferences, and even coveted swag.

Swag (sans Logo!). Speaking of swag, it is worth noting here that just because your customer loves your product or service, it doesn't mean they want to wear your logo or have it on their coffee cups. MK Getler, head of marketing of Alyce, a service that creates virtual swag stores for brands, told me in late 2020 that CMOs "ignore their research all the time by putting their logos on everything—it turns out they want the stuff but not with logos!" Because Alyce allows customers to choose their own gift when redeeming points, it is easy to test the appeal of branded versus unbranded gear. Getler reports that over 90 percent of the time, unbranded or subtly branded wins! And for the environmentally conscious, Getler reminds us that most of the branded swag that is given away ends up in the trash, creating an unnecessary environmental burden.

Before we move on to other ways to *cultivate customer champions*, allow me to tell you a story about an unforgettable yet unbranded gift I received a couple of years ago. Kerri Konik runs a boutique branding agency called Inspire Fire that Renegade engaged in 2018. We were looking to tighten up our brand story, and even though this is a service we provide to our clients, we felt the need for an outside perspective. Kerri, by the way, introduced us to Zoom, a service we adopted instantly to improve our own customer experience. But I digress. Sort of. You see, everything about working with Kerri was warm and fuzzy. Her onboarding process included a little "Inspire Fire" kit with an unbranded candle. She didn't just share results in a written report, she also provided a video recording that captured a few additional nuances. And when the project was over, she sent me an incredibly comfy unbranded plush fleece throw blanket that my wife, dog, and I snuggle under while watching TV in the winter. Simply unforgettable. No logo required.

Okay, now that we've blanketed CABs with unbranded swag, let's move on to broader reaching customer-centric initiatives.

BRINGING YOUR CUSTOMERS TOGETHER

In the pre-pandemic heyday of live events, large B2B brands brought their customers together by the thousands for multiday conferences. These events rallied customers around a common vision, educated them on the product road map, trained and certified the actual users, introduced partners in the brand ecosystem, and entertained on an occasionally epic scale. (I got to see Sheryl Crow, Train, Flo Rida, and Amy Schumer, among many others great performers, at various boondoggles—I mean, user conferences!) In my 2017 interview with Elissa Fink, then the CMO of Tableau, Fink shared how over a ten-year period, their customer events grew from two hundred people to more than thirteen thousand, an accomplishment that she found incredibly gratifying.

It wasn't just the growth of these events that made Fink proud. It was how they made their customer feel a sense of community. Attendees would tell her, "I love my job now because of Tableau. My job is so much better. You changed my life. I'm so engaged in this community." These events also created an opportunity for Fink to listen and get invaluable feedback on the product as well as the events themselves. She noted that Tableau got better at the events every year and advised people not to be held back by your mistakes or shortcomings early on.

Another brand that had tremendous success with in-person events is Salesforce.

Up until 2020, Dreamforce, Salesforce's annual user conference, was the largest representation of using events to build customer loyalty and inspire word of mouth. With more than 171,000 reported attendees in 2019, Dreamforce became a $14 billion ecosystem unto itself. Dreamforce was so big that at least one marketer, Freshworks, deployed an "ambush" campaign featuring blimps adorned with the message "#Failsforce." Noted David Thomson, then CMO of Freshworks, in our 2019 interview, "There was no better way to put ourselves on the map than to go after Salesforce, especially during Dreamforce." It is at this point that I expect you, dear reader, to say, "Hey, Drew, that's a cool story, but aren't in-person events a permanent victim of the pandemic?"

Fair question, and, in truth, it will take years for in-person events to regain their stature as the dominant means of building community. But I believe they will come back because even though some brands found success with their virtual events, engaging more people than their physical iterations at a far lower cost, virtual events fall short of the real thing on multiple dimensions. First, virtual events get only part of your audience's attention and are often in competition with email and social media. This is why so many virtual events are now only a few hours. Meanwhile, physical events essentially hold your audience captive, often for days. Second, virtual events can't (yet) replace the serendipitous opportunities for networking that naturally happen at old-fashioned conferences. Most of us humans like to be around humans, and the pent-up demand for physical experiences should not be underestimated. Mark my words, in-person events will be back, and early movers will reap the rewards. If you want your customers' undivided attention, you'll need to get them out of their #WFH cocoons.

That said, I also believe virtual events are here to stay, so it's worth reviewing some of the key lessons learned in 2020 about how to make them even better.

MAKING VIRTUAL EVENTS WORK

As you no doubt saw for yourself, all in-person conferences were canceled after March 2020, and most aren't expected to resume until 2022. The impact of these cancellations on B2B companies cannot be overstated. In addition to the revenue lost by the event organizers, millions of human-to-human interactions simply did not happen. On-site training sessions did not occur. Recruitment opportunities were lost. Serendipitous accidental meetings did not happen. Random product demos vanished. In my conversations with more than a hundred CMOs in 2020, the consensus was that *cultivating customer champions* got a whole lot harder without these events, not to mention the gaping hole it left in their lead-generation plans. As it turns out, in-person events and trade shows had represented 30 to 50 percent of its sales pipeline in 2019. So, finding a virtual replacement for physical events was not a casual undertaking but rather an urgent need.

Adobe provided one of my earlier pandemic-era experiences with a virtual event—and it did not go well. I had been on the guest list for their annual extravaganza in Las Vegas with the plan of recording podcasts with a few CMOs on the show floor. They'd already booked my hotel room and were working on my flight arrangements. The event, which would have drawn more than seventy thousand Adobe customers and partners, had been scheduled for late March. By early March, I got word the event was being canceled and to stay tuned for updates. Two weeks later, Adobe announced they would be hosting a virtual event with more than a hundred separate sessions and a kickoff presentation featuring Chelsea Handler. I watched for about an hour but was too distracted by an avalanche of email, Slack messages, and SMS texts. My thought was I'd come back to this content after other virtual attendees narrowed the list to a few must-see sessions. I never did. After the event, Adobe reported it was a success, but the buzz in the industry was less favorable.

A couple of weeks later, IBM hosted its own virtual event. Like the Adobe event, it included prerecorded and a few live sessions, a couple of which I watched with dismay. The presenters I saw were subpar, and their video connections were unstable. After about an hour, I gave up. Email won, again! It took several more months before I gave virtual conferences another chance and was delighted to see improved approaches from Skillsoft, WorkForce Software, and Sitecore.

CMO Michelle Boockoff-Bajdek (who goes by Michelle BB) and her team at Skillsoft created a global experience that rivals pre-pandemic physical events. With forty-one thousand registrants and a 34 percent attendance turnout, Skillsoft's Perspectives 2020, which included three regional (North America, Europe, and Asia) versions in one twenty-four-hour period, was a success. As BB shared in our 2020 interview, Skillsoft experimented with an entirely new model for customer presentations to ensure high engagement levels, basing presentations on an "HBR-style case study where we had a written case study for our customers and then a ten- to twelve-minute TED-style talk with the presenter and a Q&A." The response was so compelling that Skillsoft plans on testing the same model when in-person events return.

In our podcast conversation, Michelle BB shared many tips for setting up virtual events, including:

1. Assemble the right teams. Skillsoft had seven teams focused on 138 different aspects of the production. BB and her team are well versed in "agile" processes and include "scrum masters" (specially trained project managers) who ensure timely outcomes.
2. Talk to your peers. BB made a point of speaking with a number of marketers, including folks she knew at Adobe, who'd just wrapped up their own virtual event.
3. Match the tech platform with your goals. BB wanted to be able to brand all aspects of the experience, have unique content tracks, and enable one-on-one chats among attendees within these tracks.
4. Make it fun. Skillsoft's virtual summit included live entertainment, high-quality guest speakers with broad appeal, yoga breaks, and a trivia contest. BB was particularly surprised at how popular the trivia contest proved to be. Skillsoft also had a game-like points system for attendees to earn swag, which may not have been worth the trouble. About eight hundred of the fourteen thousand attendees participated in the points program.
5. Prepare for the unexpected. This advice was given to BB before the event by one of her MCs, and it proved invaluable during one technical delay. BB had prepared for just this eventuality and remained calm while smoothing over the interruption. Skillsoft also recorded all the live sessions in advance just in case the tech failed during

the real thing. Having all the content recorded was an insurance policy that BB was delighted she never had to redeem.

6. Have and support chat. Skillsoft's event followed the sun, opening first during daytime hours in Asia. As the event began, the Skillsoft team noticed higher-than-expected chat volume and quickly drafted new team members to be moderators when the event moved into the US time zones. The amount of chat blew BB and her team away as attendees shared their enthusiasm for the event in real time.

7. Give yourself an eight-to-twelve-week production runway. The Skillsoft team pulled off their event in about nine weeks, which was a minor miracle, but BB would not have wanted much more time. "If we had had more time, we might have spent a lot of it second-guessing ourselves," explained BB. More time does not necessarily mean a better event.

8. Be ready to follow up. Virtual events done right have an urgency that will attract a wide range of potential customers. The challenge is to quickly sort through the registrants and the attendees to figure out which ones are genuine leads and what is the optimal approach for nurturing these leads. Some event organizers create a scoring system based on attendee behavior. Others use polls within sessions to help identify hot prospects from warm leads. The point here is to be ready to keep the conversation going with your attendees.

9. Generate a trial with an offer. One of the more powerful ways of converting attendees into brand advocates is to give them something that can keep them engaged after the event. For Skillsoft, this meant making their courses available for free to all attendees for sixty days after the event. In doing so, Skillsoft exposes its product to a whole new group of users, many of whom will remember the brand when they are in the position to choose an education platform for their companies.

Undoubtedly, large virtual events will continue to get better as the underlying technology improves and marketers think of new ways to enhance these experiences. In the meantime, let's turn our attention to the rise of virtual microevents and how these became an important means of *cultivating customer champions* in 2020.

THE RISE OF VIRTUAL MICROEVENTS

Prior to 2020, numerous B2B brands hosted small gatherings of their high-value customers with perhaps a few hot prospects at a local restaurant or hotel. These events typically included a cocktail hour for networking, some presentations by other customers or relevant experts, and/or interesting speakers. Many included an element of entertainment (singer, magician, whiskey tasting), and a gift was provided on the way out. Sometimes called "salons," these microevents were high-touch opportunities to gather insights, thank customers for their loyalty, and give them more reason to sing your praises. Of course, these types of in-person soirees were also canceled when the pandemic struck. But interestingly, many B2B marketers found quick success during the pandemic by replicating these small events via platforms like Zoom. Chandar Pattabhiram, the CMO of Coupa, became a huge fan of virtual microevents after testing a couple of approaches. The winning mix proved to be having a small group of like-titled executives (ten to twelve maximum), a touch of entertainment, an interesting speaker, and very little product messaging. In fact, these worked out best, explained Pattabhiram, when "our customers did all of the selling." For the entertainment aspect, each attendee would be shipped an event kit, often including the wine or whiskey to be tasted that evening. "Our customers really appreciated the chance to be with their peers, and often these were the same level of executives that wouldn't have made themselves available in the pre-pandemic period," noted Pattabhiram. Other CMOs added their own twist to this approach as a means of generating leads, which we'll cover in the next section. In the meantime, let's review how you know if you've cultivated a customer champion.

How does a *cultivated customer champion* behave? Ultimately, a *cultivated customer champion* expresses brand love in all sorts of important ways:

1. They continue to buy your product/service.
2. They are keenly interested in your development road map.
3. They show up at your user conferences.
4. They evangelize about your brand to their peers offline and via social media channels.
5. They allow your company to use their brand name on your website and in sales materials.
6. They participate in case histories.
7. They provide testimonials and are willing references.

The last three areas are a challenge for new brands and companies in sensitive markets like cybersecurity. For new brands, it's harder to get testimonials sometimes because there is a reluctance among the sales or service people to ask. Seems silly, right? Nonetheless, not asking is the surest way not to have enough case histories and/or references!

There are strategic reasons your customers might not want to provide testimony. Occasionally, they'll see a particular supplier as a source of competitive advantage and simply don't want others to know. Or they see your security product as so important that they wouldn't want the bad guys to know they are using it. In theory, this should feel flattering. But most of the time, it's just making your life more difficult. Here you need to make the case that both organizations win when your company grows, since growth usually helps drive product improvements. And your growth is dependent on having top-quality case histories and references. This argument doesn't always work, but it's worth a conversation.

Here are four ways to generate B2B customer case studies and testimonials beyond what we've discussed above:

1. **Build testimonial rights and incentives into your contracts.** We've worked with some brands who offer up to a 10 percent discount to any customer who agrees to be featured as a customer on promotional materials.

Even without an offer, the best time to ask is upfront so it doesn't come as a surprise later on in the relationship.

2. **Develop a highly visible and creatively executed case history program.** If the quality (video and/or written) and visibility (promote via ads and at events) are strong enough, customers are far more likely to want to participate and will see it as a way to promote their own brand.

3. **Establish a customer-only awards program.** Just about everyone appreciates recognition and will find an awards program hard to resist. These awards can reinforce your overall brand promise, and the application process can help you gather the facts you need to produce great case histories.

4. **Attach all large clients to an executive sponsor.** Executive sponsor programs typically mean that one member of the C-suite is assigned to a particular client, often at the pitch stage, who maintains the relationship throughout. As one CMO put it: "Our clients have one throat to choke if something goes wrong, and they know who to call to get fast resolution of big issues." Having these direct client relationships makes it easier for the CMO to ask for and get a testimonial.

One of the biggest benefits of *cultivating customer champions* is that it will make your job a lot easier. Yana Nigen, CMO of JobDiva, puts it this way: "Marketing became simple in the past twelve to twenty-four months as our highest source of lead traffic comes from client referrals."

Hopefully you can see why *cultivating customer champions* is an essential step in building an unbeatable B2B brand.

KEY TAKEAWAYS

- Happy customers are the gift that keeps on giving.
- Every CMO should have at least a few key customers on speed dial.
- You know your brand is on track when you've built a community of engaged and devoted evangelists.

CHAPTER 9

SELL THROUGH SERVICE

Summary: Be a giver. Give away as much as you can, including insights, tools, swag, and maybe even product to build awareness and trust. Make it easy to buy.

Inspiration can come from anywhere. In 2006, mine came from Benjamin Franklin, and to this day, he continues to be an obsession. Having devoured dozens of books on him or by him, I can say with great certainty he was America's first chief marketing officer. After all, Franklin masterfully marketed a revolution to the French king, who ultimately funded, armed, and powered the Americans to victory. Without French support, America's chances of winning the Revolutionary War would have been slim to *ce n'est pas possible.*

That makes Franklin one of the coolest CATS ever. He was a Courageous revolutionary and an Artful communicator who often shunned the spotlight to get more done, preferring a private conversation or well-written article to a grand speech. He was Thoughtful on an epic scale, helping to establish Philadelphia's first fire station, first library, and the University of Pennsylvania, among many other enduring institutions. And no doubt about it, Franklin was Scientific, making lasting contributions to what's known about electricity. (Fun fact: Franklin coined the terms "positive," "negative," and "battery" in connection with electric charges.)

But in 2006, it wasn't Franklin's career that attracted my attention. At that time, I'd noticed a trend in which some marketing was beginning to have genuine utility versus the overt "pollution" caused by mere messaging. At this same moment, I stumbled upon Franklin's aphorism: "Well done is better than well said." Eureka! That phrase hit me like a lightning bolt. Having spent a large part of my career obsessed with words, I found myself encouraging our clients to take action, to do things that would speak louder than words, to create thoughtful programs for customers and prospects alike. Words are empty unless backed by actions. Actions are what really matter—specifically, actions that provide a service. This service mindset is at the heart of *selling through service*.

SELLING THROUGH SERVICE WRIT LARGE FOR SMALL BUSINESS

Most likely you've heard of Small Business Saturday, probably even honored it with your wallet. But maybe you've never thought of the sheer thoughtful nature of it, or how it neatly fits into the idea of *selling through service*.

Small Business Saturday is a program American Express conceived and executed in six weeks for the first time in 2010. John Hayes, who was CMO at American Express when Small Business Saturday launched, noted in our 2015 interview, "We don't do things just because they're a trend; we do things because it's the right thing to do for our customers." Since then, the program has continued to grow and evolve as it drives people to support their local businesses. In addition to calling attention to small businesses during the biggest retail weekend of the year starting with Black Friday, American Express provides marketing kits to these businesses and offers spending incentives to cardholders. With Small Business Saturday, the marketing and the service they are providing are essentially indistinguishable.

The impact of this program has risen substantially in the last eleven years. Nine in ten US consumers say Small Business Saturday has had a positive impact on their community. American Express reported that the program generated a record high of $19.8 billion in (online and offline) spending in 2020 alone, reaching a total of $143 billion since the day it began—that's $143 billion over the course of eleven days! Whether you call this *selling through service* or just plain smart marketing, the results are undeniable.

CMO HUDDLES—A PANDEMIC BABY

In mid-March 2020, I, like so many small business owners, faced an existential crisis of unprecedented proportions. Renegade's survival was by no means guaranteed. Sure, we'd weathered crises before, including 2008 when the economy collapsed, but as they say in investment ads, "past performance is no guarantee of future results." At that moment, none of us knew how bad things would get for the economy as a whole or specifically for our world of B2B marketers. But I did know that inaction was not an option and that there was a community out there that just might need our help. "Help" being the operative word.

Gathering my small leadership team for an emergency powwow, I said to them, "I don't know if we're going to get any new business in the next few months, so let's just try to make as many new friends as we can by being as helpful as we can." That was March 17. On April 1, I hosted our first huddle, a moderated conversation via Zoom with seven CMOs, three of whom were clients. Given how quickly the crisis was evolving, we elected to meet weekly, addressing new challenges as they arose and inviting other B2B CMOs who expressed interest. The conversations were intense, substantive, and occasionally therapeutic as we focused on sharing experiences, not opinions. More and more CMOs joined us each week. These sessions weren't for philosophical grandstanders but instead offered testable approaches to fresh challenges such as maintaining employee morale in a virtual workplace, creating an antiracist culture and inclusive workforce, replacing in-person events, and even building customer advisory boards without face-to-face meetings (as we covered in Chapter 8).

By August, we had fifty regular huddlers, divided into four separate huddles, one of which was only for CMOs in transition. By the end of September, I'd hosted and written recaps on fifty-five separate huddles, and it was clear that there was a unique business opportunity here. So, on October 1, 2020, we officially launched CMO Huddles as a subscription service with, of course, a clearly defined purpose: "To bring together and empower an elite group of B2B CMOs to share, care, and dare each to greatness." And sticking with the eight-word limit for purpose-driven story statements prescribed in Chapter 5, we boiled that down to: "Share. Care. Dare."

CMO Huddles is a prototypical *selling through service* initiative. It began as a free service inspired by pandemic-related challenges but is now a stand-alone unit of Renegade that continues to generate innovative and practical ideas for participants. Undoubtedly, there is also a halo effect for Renegade, generating both goodwill from our clients and interest from the industry—it's unusual for an agency, let alone a boutique like ours, to have direct access to the insights of so many elite CMOs.

As a bonus, CMO Huddles gave my own career a renewed sense of purpose: if I could help a bunch of CMOs find the courage and/or skills needed to drive purpose at their organizations, then all my hard work as a student of marketers and marketing would be profoundly rewarded.

STARTING UP YOUR SELL THROUGH SERVICE PROGRAMS

To get started on creating *sell through service* programs, you need an intimate understanding of your customers—their rational needs and their emotional state of mind.

To *sell through service*, it is essential to understand all the individuals who will have some impact on the ultimate buying decision. Most CFOs will want to understand not just the cost of your product or service but also how it will either increase revenue or decrease costs or both. If your solution involves technology, the CIO (chief information officer) or IT lead will want to understand specific requirements to implement your solution, including integration, training, staffing, and ramp-up time. The chief counsel (legal) will have their list of questions. And often, the CISO (chief information security officer) will want to understand all the security-related implications of your solution. You can save all these folks a lot of time and effort if you anticipate their information needs and preempt their homework efforts with well-crafted category assessments and comparison charts.

I realize the needs assessment described above is rudimentary, but you'd be amazed how many companies make their prospects work just to find the basics.

MAKE BUYING EASIER

One of the better-known advocates of the *selling through service* approach is Brent Adamson, a principal executive advisor at Gartner and author of two must-read bestsellers, *The Challenger Sale* and *The Challenger Customer*. The second book is most relevant to this book because, in it, Adamson points to a fundamental problem in B2B: "buying is broken."

Many big businesses have a problem buying, Adamson says. Let's say you're lucky enough to connect with a champion for your product or service inside a targeted organization. And you've armed that individual with solid proof that your solution will save their organization time and money, improve operational efficiency, and even deliver a competitive advantage. Nice job, except your sales process is just getting started.

A buying committee will now be formed, including a wide range of purchase influencers from IT, security, procurement, finance, and elsewhere. This august team will do their homework, researching vendors and preparing recommendations. Then the CEO will ask to be a part of the initiative. So, the buying committee will start again. New people get involved. Then your champion will say in the ninth month, "We just found out that our finance review committee needs to assess deals over a million dollars, and sorry, but they don't meet for two months."

Eighteen months later, even if you close the sale, the process was so arduous that many times your new customer isn't even happy with their decision.

The solution, according to Adamson, is to make buying easier by anticipating all the needs of various committee members and offering tools and content that can push your B2B brand over the finish line.

One of the benefits of *selling through service* is that it aligns with *cultivating customer champions.* By making buying easier, you are far more likely to end up with customers who are happy from the beginning and who are excited about putting the newly acquired product or service to good use. Think about your own buying experiences. The ones that were painful all the way through leave you with lingering doubts or, worse, buyer's remorse that rarely results in a willingness to express brand love. On the flip side, a frictionless buying experience often leads to customers who are more than happy to provide glowing testimonials and case studies that become pillars of your content program.

GETTING TO KNOW YOU

The *sell through service* mindset requires marketers to put customers at the center of the universe. It's human nature to put *ourselves* at the center of the universe. And even five hundred years after Copernicus disabused us of this notion, planetarily speaking, many a marketer still wants to put the spotlight on their specific product or service rather than the customers in their orbit. Don't get me wrong, the gravitational pull within the organization to talk about your brand in all its glory is huge. But as Yoda would say, "Resist this we must."

Putting your customer at the center of your content universe can be harder than you think. It means doing a lot of homework.

In my 2019 interview with Ian Howells, the CMO of Sage Intacct, a cloud-based financial software company, Howells shared how they grew their business by going after very specific market target segments, or what he called "micro-verticals." Before they opened a new micro-vertical, they would interview twenty-five to fifty people to really get to know that group's specific issues. Then they turned this research into content that demonstrated a deep understanding of the marketplace, so much so that prospects want to read their content because it is packed with useful insights.

Howells's unique approach is worth a closer look. First, he explains the need for multiple interviews:

The core thing is to interview more customers than your competitors will—to understand the market better. For example, if you think about most CFOs, if they have a problem or if they want to fix something, they probably confide in two or three other people, not fifty. If you do fifty interviews, you end up knowing more about the market than the people within the market. People stop too early. If you stop with five, thinking you know the answer, you're crazy. It's more like, at least twenty. And then you see it, when you see the same pattern occurring over and over again, the same phraseology, the same kind of pains—when you can always predict what people are going to be saying, you know that you understand the micro-vertical.

Sage Intacct goes so far as to train and certify its senior employees on interviewing so they know how to get useful information. Howells notes: "Because learning about market verticals and interviewing customers is the most important part of the company culture, the very last thing you should do is outsource it to some outside writer. This is so important that your key people should be doing this and should be really good at it. Key people, senior people, should be certified at interviewing. The worst thing you can do is A) outsource it or B) be bad at it."

How do Howells and his team get all these interviews? It's not by bribing customers with $25 Amazon vouchers, which he believes attracts the wrong interviewees. Instead, he promises to nominate them for awards, get them speaking opportunities, and get them featured in relevant press articles as a means of enhancing their careers. Howells reveals, "I think you want to have people who want to tell their stories and give them the platform to showcase the great job that they've done." The service in this case is helping prospective customers build their personal brands, and in doing so, you've started a relationship and gleaned important insights. Talk about win-win! That is the very essence of *sell through service*.

In Chapter 5, we went into detail on the importance of synthesizing your brand story into eight words or less and then taking actions to make your story real. When these actions are targeting prospects, that's how you *sell through service.* Here's a story to drive that point home.

CONNECTING THE DOTS—FROM PURPOSE TO SERVICE

For Jennifer Deutsch, CMO of Park Place Technologies, a company that specializes in maintaining third-party servers in data storage facilities, the first challenge was finding the brand story. After extensive interviews with employees and customers, Deutsch had an aha moment. When it comes to server maintenance, the only thing that matters is that they don't fail. Servers can't serve if they go down. Money is lost when servers are unintentionally under repair. Finding a positive spin for the story, the brand reduced its promise at that moment to three words: "all about uptime."

Great word choice. Concise. Relevant. Positive. Memorable. But why should customers and prospects believe these three words? Recognizing the necessity for proof, Deutsch worked with the product team to build a new AI software that could anticipate when a server would go down before it was too late. Words and actions combined. "All about uptime" became a genuine organizational commitment.

Before launch, Deutsch and her team spent several weeks explaining to all Park Place employees the inspiration behind the new campaign. This allowed their internal audiences to buy into the new direction. Then, the global external rollout followed with digital and print marketing efforts.

In all of this, Deutsch reinforced that simplicity was essential to her team's marketing efforts. It started with a simple understanding of what matters to customers, what makes them angry, and what makes them happy. After you've identified those puzzle pieces, you can begin to craft a complete program, not just messages, that speak to those needs. Park Place Technologies made what could have been an immensely technical story easy to grasp; they framed their promise with their customers' priorities in mind and then presented a state-of-the-art technical solution to seal the deal.

This is an excellent example of *selling through service*, making your promise real and in real (up) time! But it is certainly not the only way to do so. One of the most common ways these days is the creation of content, lots and lots of content.

CONTENT, CONTENT, CONTENT

The entire world of content marketing is essentially a subset of *selling through service* with a few important caveats. First, all your content should support a single brand story. Adamson's research shows that brands with a consistent story across their content are two times more likely to win than those that try to tell a different story to each of their targets. Second, a modest amount of great content is better than a deluge of mediocrity. Third, resist the temptation to make all your content about your brand, about what you do and why you're so great.

The book *Epic Content Marketing* by Joe Pulizzi focuses on the importance of creating compelling content that informs, engages, or amuses to drive behavioral change in customers and prospects. It's an excellent resource for anyone just getting into the content game, and I share Pulizzi's belief that cutting through with content is unlikely unless you have a truly unique approach—the days of easy wins with content are long gone.

So, how do you approach content when there's so much out there already? I will let Pulizzi answer before I explain more fully as it relates to *selling through service*. "To start, you need to be honest about the content you have. Most likely, your organization has plenty of feature- and benefit-related content—truly, most brands have become quite adept at talking about themselves. We clearly don't need more of that kind of content, especially when that type of information is only useful for a very small part of a buyer's journey. What brands lack are stories that engage their customers—and drive customers and prospects to take a desired action."

INVESTING IN ACTION, REMOVING FRICTION

In her role as CMO (2016–2019) of London-based Tungsten Network, Connie O'Brien took on a huge task: spearheading the first fully integrated content marketing campaign for the company and its e-invoicing platform. Since Renegade was the lead agency, we started as usual in search of the brand story. Explained O'Brien, "What we decided to do was to talk to our customers. We have a lot of data that's at our fingertips based on various research companies in the marketplace, but we needed to gather more unfiltered input."

Unfiltered input was exactly what we received. After interviews with staff, executives, partners, and customers, we determined that there was an abundance of efficiency-killing friction between buyers and suppliers when it came to issuing and paying invoices.

Recognizing that Tungsten Network's e-invoicing platform removes the bulk of this friction for many of the world's largest companies, we created a narrative structure that made "friction" enemy number one in the procurement industry. Tungsten Network, itself, was positioned as the tool to reduce this friction, in pursuit of a "frictionless future," while its customers became the heroes of the story—the "friction fighters" who make their companies more profitable and efficient by reducing invoicing friction.

To confirm that friction was indeed a global challenge for Tungsten's target audience, Renegade orchestrated the first-ever global study of P2P (procure-to-pay) friction in partnership with a leading authority in the category. This research quantified the extent of the problem and established a Friction Index that measured changes in friction over time. This research proved to be newsworthy as well, generating several dozen feature stories in business and trade pubs two years running.

To help prospects determine the level of friction in their procurement process, Tungsten also launched the Friction Finder, a free tool that exemplifies the spirit of *selling through service*. In addition to diagnosing the relative amount of friction your company was experiencing, it also offered up immediate suggestions on how to remove that friction.

During this multiyear campaign, the Tungsten blog featured real-world stories of friction-filled situations and brand videos also created by Renegade, which brought a touch of humor to the science of friction. The result of all this friction-focused content: leads, leads, and more leads. Noted O'Brien in our 2019 podcast interview, "Our sales pipeline is chock full. We have a long sales cycle, but we have not seen this many leads in a very long time. It's really important to bring everyone to the table—hearing the same message, being consistent around collaboration and roles, and rewarding good ideas."

EXTENDING YOUR SELLING THROUGH SERVICE MENTALITY TO SOCIAL MEDIA

Over the course of this book, we've referenced how various programs like State Street's *Fearless Girl* statue gained massive "free" exposure via social media. But what we've yet to do is talk about social media on its own. Part of that is by design. We believe social media works best when it is a servant to your overall brand strategy and not a tactic that stands in isolation. Another reason is that social media has been the subject of innumerable books and tends to evolve faster than you can say TikTok.

But that certainly isn't meant to imply that renegade marketers can or should neglect social media. In my September 2020 interview with Jamie Gilpin, the CMO of Sprout Social, we spent forty-five minutes together discussing several ways B2B brands can leverage social. Here's Gilpin on where social fits into her marketing efforts:

> For us at Sprout, we are mission-focused on our customers as the center point. I know every company says that, especially in B2B, especially in software and tech, but that was one thing that really attracted me to Sprout in the first place two and a half years ago when I joined. One, as a customer of Sprout prior to, but also, they're just so authentic. I mean, when we say that our customers are center point, you can see it on social, all of the #SproutLove that our customers give us. But we absolutely are always thinking about them. From a customer experience perspective, social has to be part

of every single touchpoint of our customer's journey.

I shared that whole paragraph to emphasize that success with social media starts with a service mentality, not a selling one. If you focus on service, starting with your existing customers, chances are your social media will include a sizable listening component, one in which you're receiving and responding to customer feedback in real time.

Gilpin believes social media continues to open the door for new business opportunities. Exclaiming, "We will always stand by the power of social for businesses to connect and create a real connection with their audience," Gilpin is a powerful advocate for the notion of *sell through service*. Using Sprout's listening tools, she and her team were able to identify topics that the brand should and shouldn't be supporting during the pandemic. One example she offered was the request for content around the area of managing mental health since so many social media managers were facing burnout. This insight also prompted the development of an awards program for social media managers.

BEFORE YOU CAN SELL THROUGH SERVICE

It is important to note that before you can start to *sell through service*, your organization needs to meet at least the industry standard for customer service. For example, if you're a software company and you don't offer twenty-four-seven online support like your competitors, chances are you are going to make many customers quite unhappy. No amount of marketing can reverse the reputational damage caused by subpar customer service. On the other hand, as this next story illustrates, a well-handled customer complaint can do wonders for your brand.

TWITTER BOMB TO THE RESCUE

In July 2020, after four months in test mode, it looked possible that CMO Huddles could become a stand-alone business for Renegade, so I thought we should secure a d/b/a ("doing business as" name) for it. Talking to my accountant, he suggested using LegalZoom since it wasn't necessarily a complicated process. Filling out the online forms on July 23, I received an email thank-you right away with the expectation that this process would take three to four weeks. But when I checked back three weeks later, I noticed no progress had been made. Then I tried contacting customer service via their online portal, and when that left me unsatisfied, I called their 800 number. That, too, was useless as the pandemic had stressed their ability to answer phones with any sort of regularity, and, twice, I was simply disconnected. Frustrated, I deployed my favorite nuclear option—a Twitter bomb.

Copying the CEO of LegalZoom on my carefully crafted tweet, I explained my plight and expressed my disappointment. Would you believe the CEO responded in thirty minutes, and within an hour, I'd received a customer care call from the "office of the president" escalation unit? A few minutes later, the issue was resolved, the application filed, and the d/b/a arrived four weeks later. Telling this story to Sprout Social's Jamie Gilpin on our podcast, she noted, "That is what B2B buyers are also doing with B2B companies. We see that all the time, asking about a certain feature that's about to be released or a problem that they're having and acting as customer care." The moral of the story: before you think about creating *sell through service* programs, make sure you are set up to serve your customers in a timely fashion on their channel of choice, including social media.

THE UNBEATABLE BANKCAB

The *selling through service* mindset recognizes that your marketing can provide a genuine service to your customers. It can educate. It can inform. It can inspire. It can resolve a debate. It can enhance careers. It can sell without a sales pitch.

And it can provide a laugh on a gloomy day.

One of my favorite examples of how to *sell through service* comes from the Renegade archives. Back in 2003, HSBC wanted New Yorkers to believe that it really was "The World's Local Bank" and part of the fabric of the city. So, we presented the bank with a unique program that was essentially a service, which we called the BankCab. Securing a vintage 1982 Checker Cab, once a ubiquitous symbol of the city, we then orchestrated a search for the most knowledgeable cab driver in New York City. The finals were held in front of a large press corps and ended up generating more than 120 million press impressions around the world.

Johnnie Morello won the contest and went on to give free rides and useful tips about New York City to HSBC customers for the next eleven years. In addition to delighting thousands of customers as they cruised around Manhattan at no charge, the program generated enormous word of mouth. On average, each passenger told five friends about their experience and was three times more likely to recommend HSBC than non-riders. Other components like our "Bank Cabbie Guides," written by celebrated foodie Ed Levine, helped reinforce the idea that HSBC did indeed have local knowledge that you could, well, bank on. Not surprisingly, this program garnered seven marketing awards, including a gold REGGIE for most innovative idea, a Silver Ex for best mobile marketing promotion, and Brandweek's Guerrilla Marketer of the Year accolade.

SOME CLOSING THOUGHT STARTERS

Given that I've spent the better part of the last two decades thinking about ways to turn marketing into something of value and not disruptive pollution that clutters our inboxes or airwaves, I could go on and on about both the power of *selling through service* and examples of this approach in action. My hope is that you'll leave this chapter recognizing that we're talking about a mindset. As one CMO shared in a June 2020 huddle after the success of an altruistic program designed to help their customers get through the pandemic: "The less we try to sell with our marketing, the more we seem to sell."

By this point, I hope you've thought of a bunch of ways you could *sell through service*, but just in case, here are several other thought starters:

- A PR-worthy proprietary research study on the future of your industry

- A buyer's guide to your category with (relatively) unbiased reviews of your top competitors
- An ROI calculator
- A maturity model that helps prospects determine where they stand relative to the state of the art
- An app that enables prospects to do some aspect of their job more easily
- A wellness program for your target's employees
- A free shuttle from a hotel to your conference
- An exclusive high-quality event (virtual or in person when that's possible)

KEY TAKEAWAYS

- Marketing, like karma, is a boomerang, so focus on helping your prospects.
- If you want to sell more, turn your marketing into something of genuine value.
- Make sure your social channels are set up to serve first.

PART IV

SCIENTIFIC METHOD

Even the most courageous, artful, and thoughtful renegade marketer will fail without this last trait: be scientific. Part of this failure will be perception, in that these first three traits are often seen as fuzzy relative to words like "sales," "revenue," "ROI," "CAC" (customer acquisition cost), and "growth." C-suites and boards of directors tend to be populated with data-driven individuals, folks who like to chart progress with facts and figures. The CMO who doesn't know how to translate marketing-speak into financial-speak is unlikely to be taken seriously. The other part of the failure will be reality. Without hard data that shows forward progress and backs up why you chose one direction instead of another, you the marketer will be you the job seeker in short shrift.

My choice of the word "scientific" rather than, say, "mathematical" or "data-driven" is not just because those terms wouldn't have yielded the memorable CATS acronym. CATM? CATD? Forgettable, for sure. In truth, I use the word "scientific" because it takes us to the all-important scientific method, which can be boiled down to making observations and doing experiments, essentially testing your way to success. The process starts by setting the right benchmarks (Chapter 10: Measure What Matters). This is followed by deploying highly effective marketing technologies while making sure you're not over-investing (Chapter 11: Automate Attentively). Then we conclude with a personal and organizational mandate for continuous improvement (Chapter 12: Test to Triumph). The cool CATS you've read about in this book are always experimenting, recognizing that what works for them today may not work tomorrow.

CHAPTER 10

MEASURE WHAT MATTERS

Summary: Work with your CFO and data chief to develop metrics that matter for employee satisfaction, customer advocacy, and prospect interest.

Businesses are often defined by the metrics that matter most to the CEO and board of directors. Enron famously focused on top-line revenue growth and stock valuation, so much so that it led to a culture of making sales at all costs and bookkeeping tricks. That story didn't end well for anyone involved.

A CMO that is only measured (and rewarded) for leads generated will naturally care more about quantity and less about quality and very little about anything else. Even if that metric is shifted to revenue generated, the CMO is far less likely to have interest in longer-term success factors like culture, reputation, customer experience, or retention rates.

It is not unusual for me to hear a CMO proclaim that revenue is the only metric that matters to their organization, which helps explain why more than 80 percent of B2B budgets are allocated to acquisition-related activities. Because you are what you measure, we better be darn sure we're *measuring what matters*. Since there are innumerable data points available today, this chapter will zero in on a few must-haves in the measurement department.

MEASUREMENT HIGHLIGHTS MARKETING VALUE

In this chapter, we will cover the role of measurement in the success of your marketing efforts. Beyond helping you achieve your marketing program goals, however, measurement has another important role for marketers: reinforcing the relationship of marketing with the CEO and other parts of the organization. Measurement is key in setting two cornerstones that need to be in place from the beginning to ensure your success as a CMO.

First, if you're the head of marketing, you can't even think about trying new things without the express support of your CEO. Ironically, this is where many CMOs fail, and it happens often before they even start their jobs. You might be scratching your head here wondering how a CMO could fail before they even begin.

It's easy. Many CMOs fail because they are misaligned with the expectations of their respective CEOs. Setting expectations is so important that it was the opening element in my first book, featuring an interview with Jeffrey Hayzlett, the founder of the C-Suite Network and former CMO of Kodak. Hayzlett notes that "a lot of CMOs fail because they forget to get the *conditions* of satisfaction" (emphasis mine). In other words, they have not nailed down the key measures of success and therefore will have little chance of demonstrating the value of their contributions. This seems like an obvious thing, but you'd be surprised how few marketers have metrics of success in place at the start of their new positions.

The second critical cornerstone for any CMO is a basic understanding of the role marketing currently plays within the organization. Companies like P&G, Unilever, and PepsiCo are well known for being marketing driven, meaning that marketers control strategy and often have P&L (profit and loss) responsibilities. If you control the P&L, then you can test variables, most famously the four P's (product, promotion, price, placement), and you can think about marketing and your role quite broadly.

This is rarely the case in B2B organizations, which are more likely to be driven by engineers, sales, or finance. Here, the marketer often faces less receptive cultures, being seen as a luxury by executives who may have little understanding of how marketing works. In these situations, it is even more important that you the marketer set expectations, delineating not just the role of marketing within the organization but also how performance should be measured.

Part of the problem is that despite the massive shift to digital marketing, the rise of data analytics, marketing automation, account-based marketing, and even artificial intelligence, marketing effectiveness remains remarkably hard to measure. This is particularly true for marketers targeting large enterprises, which typically have yearlong sales cycles and multiple decision-makers, thus making it next to impossible to connect any one of the marketing components to the ultimate sale. With these challenges in mind, let's discuss how you can indeed *measure what matters*.

MEASURE CUSTOMER DELIGHT BY THEIR ACTIONS

Next up in our pursuit to *measure what matters*, we need to focus on your customers. In Chapter 8, we discussed the need to *cultivate customer champions* and the critical role customer happiness plays not just in maintaining your business but also in helping it grow. If customers don't believe in the changes you've made to your brand, then you certainly can't expect prospects to respond favorably either.

NPS, as discussed earlier, has been touted as the only number you need to measure customer satisfaction (c-sat). For a few companies, this might be true, but for most of the CMOs I've interviewed, it is entirely insufficient. Among the problems with NPS is that it measures stated intent only and not actions. Likelihood to recommend is not the same as a referral, a written recommendation, a case study, a contract renewal, or an increase in contract size. As a baseline measure, NPS certainly has value, particularly if you have a low score relative to your industry (that means you have customer experience issues that need to be identified and fixed). Just don't stop there.

As an alternative, or to buttress NPS, consider developing your own blended "mega-metric" for c-sat. Blended metrics have numerous advantages. First, you aren't relying on just one measure to reveal "truth." Second, you get to combine the factors you consider most important and weight them. Third, blended metrics won't overwhelm your brain and those with whom you share data—it is a common complaint of boards that CMOs share too much data and not the data that matters. Your blended customer satisfaction score can be created from a range of data points like:

- Referrals: percentage of customers who provide referrals
- References: percentage of customers who are willing to provide references
- Case studies: percentage of customers who are willing to participate in case studies
- Renewals: percentage of customers gained in one year that renewed the next
- Upsells: percentage of customers who bought more of your services after one year
- Training: percentage of customers who are certified on your software
- Events: percentage of customers who attend your user conferences each year

To create your c-sat mega-metric, pick five of the metrics above, add up the percentages, and then divide by five. Or these can be weighted depending on the business goals of the organization. Regardless of the exact formula, you should end up with a more accurate look at the business impact of your new brand strategy and related marketing activities on your current customer base. One bonus from this approach is that it puts extra value on customers who are willing to take action on your behalf, even if they aren't the biggest or fastest-growing customers. These customers have a different kind of value that is helpful to reflect in your effort to *measure what matters*.

AppsFlyer's Ran Avrahamy is a proponent of a single customer-related metric. "For our clients, our main metric is their success," Avrahamy says. "We measure how successful our clients are in their space, and how well they are using our platform. Revenue is, and always has been, secondary."

REACHING FOR REACH

"Hall of Fame" marketers like Antonio Lucio, the former CMO of Facebook, HP, and Visa, know that measurement is critical even if it tells only part of the story. I interviewed Lucio when he was CMO at Visa Inc., and he pointed to three key metrics that are equally relevant for B2B marketers: reach, brand health, and usage lift.

Reach, according to Lucio, is the sum of marketing impressions, including earned, owned, and paid media. In aggregate, reach represents the amount of exposure a brand has with its target audience, exposure that is ultimately critical to purchase decisions.

If you have any doubt about the importance of reach, I highly recommend you add *How Brands Grow* by Byron Sharp to your reading list. In his convention-challenging book, Professor Sharp shows a direct correlation between brand penetration, market share, and brand awareness. Particularly true for mass targeted brands, Sharp even makes the case that overtargeting is a mistake since light users can often have a greater impact on sales growth than heavy users who are unlikely to change their behavior based on marketing!

To put reach into context, imagine you're a new software company trying to entice large organizations to pilot your "revolutionary" new service. Even if you have unquestionable performance superiority and a very quick ROI (aka "speed to value"), just getting in the door will be next to impossible. No doubt your sales team will be thwarted by the refrain, "If you're so great, why haven't I heard of you?" Now imagine you're calling from Salesforce, Adobe, or Oracle. Closing the sale may still be a challenge for these behemoths, but they are far more likely to gain consideration. Reach, and the awareness it generates, matters.

So, the question becomes, how many people do you need to reach to hit your sales goals? If you are Case Paper and your primary target is printers and that universe is less than ten thousand, then your reach could be every paper buyer at every printer in America. But these aren't the only potential customers. Art directors can specify paper selection, as can brand-side package designers. And then there are influencers like trade publication writers. Now, your reach is more like a hundred thousand. One way or another, you have to define the pool of people you want to reach. These folks are your target audience, and building awareness among them needs to be a top priority. As noted earlier, it's very hard to sell even an inherently awesome product or service if it has little to no awareness.

Chandar Pattabhiram, CMO of Coupa, a public company that continues to grow rapidly even during the pandemic, is another believer in the importance of awareness building. In a recent interview, Chandar shared why his marketing budget included TV advertising on programs like CNBC and how he measures it, noting, "We shifted from being a great company to a great brand and being more mainstream." Acknowledging that there was benefit for a public company to have broad-based awareness, he also noted that this channel was a good way to gain recognition among their primary target of CFOs. From a metrics perspective, Chandar measures TV's impact via Coupa's brand health studies and changes in site traffic.

NO REACH, NO AWARENESS, NO DEAL

When Kevin Sellers became CMO of Ping Identity in August of 2019, the software security company was well beyond start-up phase, with over $200 million in annual revenue. But Sellers shares that it was "not growing at the rate it could, mostly because it was still so unknown." His mandate? "One of the big things they were looking for was somebody that could come in and really help to find a brand platform and strategy and really help drive them into the much broader awareness of the technology they deliver," explains Sellers. Just how important is awareness? I'll let Sellers explain:

> It's interesting because I don't think people appreciate what awareness does. It's not a vanity play. What awareness does is, especially in a B2B world where awareness actually gets you into the short list, you can't win business if you don't even get a chance to

bid on the deal. Initially, it plays into the demand that way, but it also does so much as a multiplier to your demand-gen efforts.

If you show up at the door, knock on the door, and say, "I've got this really cool product, will you buy it?"—yeah, you'll sell a few. But if you're showing up at the door and people know who you are and a lot about what you are all about and you say, "I've got this really special thing I want to sell you," your effectiveness goes way up.

It's not just about being more known. It's about making that funnel much bigger and ensuring that your demand activities are more effective as a result.

To solve Ping's awareness problem, Sellers took a somewhat old-school approach (spokesperson-driven videos) with a few important modern-day twists. First, he *dared to be distinct* by repositioning the brand as "identity champions" and later hired athlete/actor/motivational speaker Terry Crews as their "chief identity champion." As Sellers explains, "Terry is just this infectiously optimistic, very positive, high-energy person who is a champion himself—a Super Bowl champion and a champion of a number of very important causes." The Crews "chief identity" videos, which you can find on YouTube or PingIdentity.com, are both memorable and distinctive from the usual FUD-infused (fear, uncertainty, and doubt) messages used to sell security products.

The results? Video views skyrocketed as employees, customers, and prospects liked and shared what they saw. Site traffic increased dramatically, and engagement rates with content improved. And prospective customers noticed, saying things like, "I love your spots. I'm laughing. You're so different from your competitors." One prospect told Ping's CEO, "Hey, we want to do business with you. We want to engage you. Can you connect me to the right people because we want to have 'sweet secure digital experiences'?" This turned out to be a direct reference to what Crews says in all of the videos.

What's also important about this story is that Sellers freely admits that great positioning alone didn't move the needle. Six months before they released the Crews videos, Ping started talking about the idea of being "identify champions." And while they saw some improvement in engagement scores, leads weren't flowing in the way they were after the Crews campaign launched. Sellers's conclusion?

> At the end of the day, what are we trying to do as marketers anyway? What we're really trying to do with advertising specifically is to rent a little space in the mind of your buyer. Ultimately, you're trying to get them to know you and remember you, and you can't do that by being really safe, especially when they're bombarded with messages every day. That's all of those pieces coming together and then just the great performance of Terry Crews. It's very memorable.

FROM REACH TO BRAND HEALTH

B2B CMOs, especially those at venture-backed software companies, are a clever lot. When joining their peers in the C-suite or when presenting to their investors or boards, you will rarely hear them utter the word "brand" or tie a budget item to "brand building." Instead, they deploy various euphemisms like "corporate marketing," "category creation," "making noise in the marketplace," "competitive positioning" and "messaging." Chandar Pattabhiram, whom we met earlier, deftly labels everything his department does as "revenue marketing," thus avoiding the topic of branding altogether. The reason for all this side-stepping is an unfortunate and broadly held association of the word "brand" with wasteful spending on non-revenue-driving activities. Several CMOs told me recently that their CEOs associate "brand" with logos and colors, things too trivial to be discussed by serious business professionals. With that kind of myopia, it's no wonder that very few B2B companies bother to measure the health of their brand.

WHY BOTHER MEASURING BRAND HEALTH?

Earlier in this chapter, I mentioned Antonio Lucio's three key metrics: reach, brand health, and usage lift. Reach, as we've discussed at length, ends up driving awareness and hopefully brand interest. And usage lift, as we'll learn later in this chapter, is another way of saying "revenue growth," the business objective most often favored by the C-suite. So, you might ask, what the heck is brand health and why bother measuring it when the C-suite doesn't really care?

In answer to the first questions, we're going to—for the purposes of this conversation—conjoin basic brand awareness tracking with other brand-related metrics (purchase intent, likability, trust, etc.) into something we'll agree to call "brand health tracking." As for the second and very fair question about why measuring brand health is important, allow me to tell you another story.

DEFENDING AGAINST OUTSIDE FORCES

One of the unique challenges of being a CMO is that external factors well beyond your control can have a dramatic impact on the results of your marketing efforts. For example, you could oversee marketing at a bank that is fined $185 million by the Consumer Financial Protection Bureau for creating fraudulent savings and checking accounts. That really did happen to a CMO I know. Or let's say a pandemic comes along and temporarily wipes out your entire industry, as was the case for Meagen Eisenberg, the CMO of TripActions, a cloud-based service that helps businesses manage travel expenses. While Eisenberg is a master at building demand-generation engines, she had nothing in her playbook that could overcome the brutal reality of a more than 90 percent decline in travel bookings in mid-2020.

Obviously, the pandemic is an extreme case that hopefully none of us will have to deal with again. But there are other outside forces that most marketers will face in their careers, like an economic downturn. In a typical recession, a declining tide lowers just about every boat. To no one's surprise, it's harder to drive sales when demand is down and budgets are tight. And just to make sure the CMO's job is that much harder, most companies cut their marketing budgets at the mere sniff of a downturn. Smaller market plus smaller budget is rarely the formula for success, *but* it is one that can be fought if you have a brand health study in place. Hooray! We're back to the point of all this: brand health tracking is both an offensive and defensive weapon for the renegade marketer.

With brand health tracking in place, you'll be able to measure the impact of your marketing efforts that may not show up in lead generation or revenue stats (sales is often a lagging indicator for B2B brands with long sales cycles). If your brand awareness is low among your target audience, you'll have a stronger argument for spending money on reach-generating efforts. If your target is aware of your brand but doesn't show a preference, then you'll know it's time to rethink or at least refresh your messaging. If your target is delaying purchases right now because of the economic situation, then you know you'll need to rethink your product mix and perhaps develop a lower-cost version that your target can afford. Basically, a brand-health-tracking study shines a bright light on the intangibles that can prevent purchase. ("I don't know your brand," "I don't trust your brand," etc.)

Sold yet? Would it help if there were a way to do this on the cheap? Read on.

MEASURING AWARENESS WITHOUT A TRACKING STUDY

When I worked on packaged-goods brands like Listerine, Lubriderm, and Sinutab as an account exec at JWT back in the 1980s, having a brand-tracking study in place was standard practice. Measuring things like unaided and aided awareness, recalled brand attributes, and purchase intent relative to key competitors, these semiannual studies were a critical part of the agency's performance reviews. Nearly four decades later, I'm always flabbergasted when sizable B2B brands don't have similar tracking studies in place. But I shouldn't be by now. Of the hundreds of B2B CMOs I've spoken with, less than 20 percent budget for brand-tracking studies.

Rather than lament how so few B2B marketers have these kinds of studies in place, let's assume they just can't get budget approval and focus instead on proxy measures. The idea here is that as your awareness rises, so, too, will a range of easily measurable elements of your marketing mix. For example, as more people learn about your product or service through various marketing activities, you can typically expect organic site traffic to rise. If it doesn't, you have a problem. Thus, a change in site traffic becomes a proxy for a change in brand awareness.

There are several other proxies that, when combined, can give you a pretty clear picture of whether or not your marketing is driving awareness. Let's call this the Blended Brand Awareness Tracker:

- Site traffic
- Searches of your brand name on Google
- Mentions of your brand name on social media
- Follower growth on social media
- Cost per click for your paid search ads (awareness of brand impacts clicks)
- Number of reviews on comparison sites (like G2, Capterra, etc.)
- Responsiveness to sales calls (call-per-meeting ratio)

All of these can be measured and tracked over time with a range of sophisticated tools, some of which we'll cover in the next chapter. It's also possible to track these proxies for awareness manually, albeit tediously, on a spreadsheet.

MEASURING BRAND HEALTH ON THE CHEAP

The cheapest way to measure brand health is to expand the proxy approach described above for measuring brand awareness. The biggest difference is that we're considering competitive activity a bit more. For example, instead of just monitoring searches of your brand name on Google, you compare the searches of your brand name to that of your top competitors. This would give you a proxy for share of voice. Here is a list of proxies you could measure to get some sense of brand health. Let's call this the Blended Brand Health Tracker:

- Percentage of category searches of your brand name on Google relative to your competitors
- Percentage of mentions of your brand name on social media
- Percentage of positive mentions of the brand on social media
- Share of positive reviews on product comparison sites
- Share of media mentions (many B2B brands use Meltwater for this)
- Follower growth on social media (relative to your competitors' follower growth)

Admittedly, these don't really get you the kind of insights that a true brand-health-tracking study provides. But you did ask for something cheap!

FIELD THE DAMN STUDY

The next level is an actual research study that goes out at least once a year. To make the most of a proprietary research study, I encourage you to consult with a research professional. They should be able to draft the right questions and help you find the most cost-effective way of fielding this research. The biggest driver of costs will be the size of your target audience and the degree of difficulty in reaching them. To that end, it is worth noting that several polling services have sprouted up that can field studies quickly and quite inexpensively. (We've used Pollfish and Propeller Insights and have heard good things about Quantilope.)

Before we leave brand health tracking behind, allow me to impress upon you its value in a slightly different manner. If you don't have it and there is an external marketplace disruption way beyond your control like, say, a pandemic, how will you assess and defend your marketing activities? In this scenario, brand tracking acts as an important source of truth, separating the out-of-your-control factors (i.e., recession, pandemic) from the in-your-control factors (message and medium). Otherwise, you are likely to hear a variation of "marketing is clearly not working, we need to cut the budget and, oh yeah, you should update your résumé."

FROM REACH TO BRAND HEALTH TO REVENUE GROWTH

And now, we can discuss Antonio Lucio's third golden metric: usage lift. For Visa, usage lift is easy to track since they get credit card transaction data in real time. This enables them to compare usage minute to minute, year over year, and all points in between. In the world of B2B marketing, usage lift is typically replaced with the words "revenue growth," a bucket that includes new customer revenue as well as current customer revenue increases. And in my experience, CMOs who don't try to measure marketing's impact on revenue are CMOs who won't be in their positions for an extended period.

Not that measuring marketing's impact on revenue is easy; nor, perhaps more importantly, is it cheap. As you'll learn in the next chapter, building a marketing technology (aka MarTech) system (aka "stack") that tracks leads all the way through the purchase journey can cost thousands of dollars in both licenses and time of staff. But, at the risk of repeating myself, every CMO must try to equate their collective marketing activities with a revenue-generating outcome and a return-on-marketing spend. If you're not sure where to start, my suggestion is you talk to your CFO and explain your ambition and need for his or her assistance. With this approach, you've signaled to the CFO that you acknowledge both their expertise and influence—influence that will undoubtedly boomerang as good karma when budgets are reviewed in the boardroom.

These conversations should produce mutually acceptable formulas for measuring the impact of marketing on revenue growth. Here are a few of these types of metrics and the formulas used:

CAC (customer acquisition cost)—CAC is commonly used by venture-funded B2B firms with rapid growth trajectories. In its simplest form, CAC represents the total marketing and sales expense divided by the number of customers acquired in a given period. For example, if your total costs were $2,000 and you acquired two customers, then your CAC would be $1,000. One problem with CAC is that it tells only part of the story, which is why it is often paired with the next metric.

LTV (lifetime value)—LTV is the estimated average lifetime dollar value of a customer. For example, if your customers stay with you for three years on average and spend $1,000 per year, then their LTV is $3,000. Since not all that revenue is profit, and it is often hard to project how long customers will stay in the future, some CFOs might ask you to discount your LTV both on the dollar spend and the retention period. Be prepared to debate these figures, but in the end, make sure you get agreement on the basis for LTV.

LTV:CAC ratio—In some circles, this is the magic formula. Using the examples above, we had an LTV of $3,000 and a CAC of $1,000, which produces a three-to-one ratio. In VC circles, you've done your job well and your marketing is considered optimized. If the ratio is higher than three, it means you could probably boost spending to drive more revenue. If it is below three, then your marketing approach, if not the potential of the business, will be questioned.

NNL (net new logo)—Here we are just focused on the number of new customers that marketing and sales have acquired in each period. This number is especially helpful when a brand is taking a "land and expand" approach, putting more value on getting started than the actual value of any deal.

SQL (sales qualified leads)—Here we are attempting to differentiate between any name or email address captured and a true business opportunity. In many organizations, there is a process by which MQLs (marketing qualified leads) are validated by the sales team and thus become sales qualified leads. In theory, since each SQL started as an MQL, this becomes a great starting place for calculating the next metric.

MSP (marketing-sourced pipeline)—This is a metric that many B2B CMOs brandish with pride. For example, Sprout Social's Jamie Gilpin, whom we met in Chapter 9, noted in our interview that "more than 80 percent of our new business acquisition actually comes from marketing." MSP combines SQLs, those leads we have already established were originated by marketing, and additional leads that marketing played some part in influencing (newsletters opened, webinar attended, etc.). The formula is finished by calculating the marketing-sourced leads in the pipeline versus the total, which includes those directly generated by a salesperson.

MSR (marketing-sourced revenue)—You might say we saved the best for last, if we define "best" as the one most likely to bring a smile to your CEO's and CFO's faces. Here we're tracking marketing-generated leads all the way through to a completed transaction and then dividing the marketing-sourced portion of revenue by all the revenue gained in a particular period.

CREATING YOUR DASHBOARD

I'm not suggesting that you need all the metrics we've covered in this chapter. But you do need to have a few go-to metrics that you can track and defend with the help of your CFO and ideally your head of sales. In the SiriusDecisions 2020 Metrics Study, Forrester noted that CMOs around the world limited their top-level dashboards to eight metrics on average. Why so few when we know there are hundreds of options? Because attention spans are short and C-suite execs have a lot of other things to worry about. The trick, advises Forrester, is "to stick with a crisp set of metrics that summarize marketing's value, as opposed to investing time exploring interesting—but less consequential—details."

For your reference, the SiriusDecisions 2020 Metrics Study revealed that 48 percent of B2B CMO dashboards include a sourcing metric like marketing-sourced revenue (35 percent) and marketing-sourced pipeline (32 percent). Forrester notes the inherent weakness of over-emphasizing sourcing metrics since they don't reflect retention success and since sourcing rates seem to be declining. Importantly, Forrester reports "that high-growth companies focus more on the customer life cycle." These metrics include LTV, retention rates, c-sat, and customer advocacy. Blending Forrester's guidance along with that gleaned from hundreds of CMO interviews, here are my suggestions for a solid metrics dashboard for the renegade marketer:

Employees	Customers	Prospects	Brand Health
Blended e-sat	Blended c-sat	CAC	Blended brand awareness
New employee conversion rate	LTV	MSP	Blended brand health

Because measurement and marketing technology are so deeply intertwined, this is the perfect place to pause our discussion on the need to *measure what matters* and dive into the automation that enables measurement.

KEY TAKEAWAYS

- Gain alignment with your CEO on the metrics that matter before you start.
- Create a dashboard of no more than eight metrics for your executive team.
- Include metrics that focus on employee and customer success, not just acquisition.

CHAPTER 11

AUTOMATE ATTENTIVELY

Summary: MarTech is only as good as the staff that uses it. Master one before adding another. Keep all-in costs below 10 percent of marketing budget.

MarTech is short for marketing technology, a vast category of automation tools that marketers deploy in pursuit of several magic bullets:

- Measuring the impact of every dollar spent
- Measuring the impact of every piece of content
- Measuring the impact of every prospect interaction
- Measuring the impact of an individual offer, message, image, etc.
- Measuring the impact of a combined set of interactions
- Separating real potential buyers from tire kickers
- Providing a personalized web experience

That's a lot of magic bullets, so it's little wonder that many CMOs now have larger tech budgets than their IT counterparts. The annual spending is in the billions and is growing by double digits every year. In theory, all this MarTech spending should be helping to make measurement more precise and to make marketing more effective. But that's not the case. In fact, it may be the opposite.

MONEY WELL SPENT?

A 2019 study by Forrester research pointed to the fact that despite a dramatic increase in MarTech spending, marketers were seeing little improvement in their customer-experience scores. Decrying "digital customer experiences that all look and feel the same," Forrester recommends shifting a whopping $19 billion previously earmarked for technologies to more creative efforts to gain $10 billion more in ROI over the next six years.

Forrester's assessment is easy to understand. Extra spending on MarTech often leaves less in the budget for content creation or paid media, two marketing components that can have a meaningful impact on performance. Better content typically correlates to more site traffic, more time on the website, more downloads, more qualified leads, and a shift in brand perceptions. And more paid media means more individuals will become aware of your company.

MICRO-MESSAGES VERSUS BRAND STORY

Because MarTech enables the testing of every possible variation of copy and images, often the big brand idea is lost in favor of micro-messages. These micro-messages might win a head-to-head click rate test versus a message that aligns with the overall consistent brand story.

As you might recall from Chapter 9, sending different messages to different members of your target hurts your cause. In fact, brands with a consistent story are 2.2 times more likely to close a B2B sale than those companies that send unique messages to the various members of the buying committee. Consistency really matters, a factor that the micro-messaging enabled by MarTech rarely considers.

In addition, click rates are poor measures of success. As noted earlier, not all clicks are equal, and more importantly, clicks are not the goal. The goal is to get the right people to your website and then help them any way you can in their quest for information and guidance.

You've probably heard the term "clickbait." These are digital ads featuring dancing dogs, listicles (like "10 Ways to Look 10 Years Younger"), or slideshows of what the child stars of the '80s look like today. Admittedly, these posts are often irresistible. But they rarely support an overarching brand story, and they rarely attract the right person to your website.

I'm not saying that your digital ad team is going to deploy irrelevant clickbait just to get people to your website, even though you can see how they can be easily tempted down this rabbit hole. However, they are more than likely to optimize for the wrong behavior since they have ready access to click-through data, but not to related sales data, given how long it takes to get from a lead to a sale.

SO, HOW DO YOU AUTOMATE ATTENTIVELY?

Let's start with some basics. Every B2B company should have some fundamental MarTech tools starting with a CRM system. Salesforce is the dominant player in this category, but there are many other options, some of which are focused on vertical industries or business sizes. HubSpot, for example, is a leading CRM provider among small- and medium-size businesses. At a minimum, these systems help you build and manage your database of prospects and customers. Most can do a lot more than that, assuming you have the staff to support them.

And here's where so many marketers go wrong. They overinvest in the tools and underinvest in the staff required to optimize performance. A CRM system works only if all leads are entered into the system. Email and other content-management systems work only if you invest in creating content and have individuals who can assess campaign results.

To *automate attentively*, you need to make sure you bake staffing costs into the overall budget for each tool you acquire. Before you add an additional tool, make sure you're getting the most out of the ones that you have. To do that, you need to have a clear understanding of what the tool can do for you and how you will track performance. It sounds simple enough, but you'd be shocked to know how many marketers are long on software and short on the staff needed to make the software sing. Don't be that guy.

STAFF PROPERLY

Eric Eden, most recently the CMO at Postclick, has led marketing for several brands that had spectacular exits (like going public or being acquired), including Cvent, Socrata, and hCentive. At each of these companies, Eden built sophisticated MarTech stacks that helped identify high-value leads and quantify marketing's contribution to sales. As such, he has very specific advice when it comes to staffing, explaining, "The old IT adage was for every dollar in license, it costs three dollars in staff time to implement it, and I found that that's at least the case with these types of systems." Warns Eden, "Don't be fooled when it's called marketing automation, because you need a team who is there to configure it, to run it, to manage it."

Eden goes on to describe the unanticipated reality that marketing automation may create more work for your teams. He explains, "Instead of just sending people emails one at a time, you're going to plan out the entire six months of emails they're going to get. But guess what? To do that, you have to come up with six months of content and get everyone to understand what that is." Hopefully, you get the idea here. Any tool, even one as simple as a saw, is useless without a person to use it, and preferably someone who is skilled at its application.

BUDGETING FOR MARTECH

It's not uncommon for the CMOs I interview to have more than twenty-five different marketing technologies. These are typically large businesses with a tremendous amount of site traffic. For example, back in 2018, MongoDB averaged more than forty-five thousand downloads of its free database software every single day. That's a lot of site traffic. Meagen Eisenberg, whom we met briefly in Chapter 10, was CMO of MongoDB when we talked in 2018, and noted that their tech stack was twenty-eight products high, down from thirty-five the previous year. Eisenberg was proud to have sunsetted seven that were no longer serving a meaningful role.

With so much site traffic, the challenge for Eisenberg was multidimensional. First, she wanted to know the source of the traffic to help guide future spending. Then she needed help distinguishing potential paying customers from all the free downloaders. From there, MarTech would help determine what series of content and offers could convert these leads into paying customers. There's a lot more to this story (the whole interview is on our podcast episode "The Key to Achieving Sales and Marketing Alignment in B2B"), but the point remains the same: MarTech isn't marketing. MarTech is a means of capitalizing on your marketing activities.

One rule of thumb is to keep your MarTech costs well below 10 percent of your overall marketing budget. This leaves more than 90 percent for actual marketing activities like creating content, orchestrating events, and spending on media.

CONDUCTING A MARTECH AUDIT

There's no wrong time to conduct a MarTech audit unless, of course, you've just done one or just started building up your stack. The goal is to figure out which ones are adding value, which ones are consuming more resources than they're worth, and if there are any obvious holes in the stack. Here's a suggested step-by-by approach to this audit:

1. **List:** Make a list of all the tech in your stack along with expected function, cost, and the time staff dedicate to using it.
2. **Understand:** Compare what the tools are supposed to be delivering versus the reality.
3. **Evaluate:** Compare relative value of all the tools and identify the biggest time wasters.
4. **Organize:** Map the tools in relationship to each other and your customer life cycle.

5. **Trim:** Eliminate the ones that are not making a significant difference.
6. **Explore:** Review new tech that can fill in major gaps identified during the audit.
7. **Communicate:** Share the results of the audit with your organization, including sales, marketing, IT, security, and finance.

THE UPSIDE OF MARTECH

Having warned you against overspending on MarTech, I'm now comfortable noting its enormous upside, such as identifying a site visitor in real time and serving up content that is particularly relevant to that individual yet still on-brand. It's the B2B equivalent of Netflix greeting you with movies or shows you might like to watch based on your past viewership. There are many other good reasons to increase your use of MarTech, especially if your guiding principle is how these tools can be of service to your employees, customers, and prospects.

Let's say you're an engineer at a wind-power facility paying a visit to GE.com as you consider upgrading or expanding your wind farm. Chances are, you've visited the site before, so they know who you are. Assuming the right MarTech is in place, GE can serve up highly relevant content that speaks to you the engineer like spec sheets, engineering reports, and even tutorials on extending the value of existing machines. The website does this in real time. It's not creepy; it's state-of-the-art thoughtfulness.

When you visit a website, you want relevant information. For a marketer, being relevant is the same as being thoughtful. I am confident I don't need to see ads for entry-level jobs anymore, and when that happens, it wastes my time and someone else's money. With digital marketing and the right tech, there is really no excuse for being irrelevant.

Properly configured MarTech systems not only help you be timelier and more relevant, but also improve your ability to measure the effectiveness of these efforts. Put another way, timeliness plus relevance equals measurably effective marketing. And that, dear readers, is why the coolest CATS in marketing are *automating attentively*.

HOW DOES YOUR STACK STACK UP?

If you're not familiar with The Stackies: Marketing Tech Stack Awards, I invite you to look at the forty-eight marketing stack entries from 2019 on ChiefMartec.com. Not only were they visually explosive and artfully constructed, but they also painted the picture of companies who were tech savvy within their marketing infrastructures.

To get a quick understanding of what a tech stack looks like, review the award-winning configuration from Esri, a mapping technology software provider. You will find twenty-four different tech providers divided into six cleverly named groupings: Productivity Pass, Communication Delta, Acquisition Bay, Nurturing Cove, Retention Ridge, Insights, and Analytics Viewpoint.

By the way, Esri's nomenclature and geographic visualization, though not industry standard, have the dual benefit of making the content more interesting while aligning with the brand's overall promise, "the science of where." Though we're talking automation right now, it is worth highlighting that even award entries are an opportunity to *dare to be distinct* and *delight by design*.

Another award-winning tech stack in 2019 was from Juniper Networks, one that will give a deeper understanding of how complex these systems can really get for B2B companies. Their graphic representation features more than fifty different technologies clustered into three broad "clouds" of customer life-cycle stages, including pre-sales marketing, pre- and post-sales marketing, and post-sales marketing. The tools are then sorted into five purposeful layers: management, content and experience, relationship and social, data, and sales. What is particularly interesting is that Juniper Network's tech stack is a hybrid of almost all the major MarTech enterprise companies (Microsoft, Adobe, Salesforce, SAP, Oracle), which reveals a preference for best of breed in any given application area versus a one-stop-shop approach.

STARTING YOUR STACK

We established Eric Eden's credentials a few pages back as someone who is furiously committed to having the right stack in place. Eden insists, "If you don't have a good marketing technology stack that enables your demand-generation engine, everything falls apart. And I think that happens in a couple of ways. First of all, your own team can't even measure or manage what's working and what's not working. The second thing is that you lose alignment with your sales team, your internal customer, and you lose credibility with the other people on the management team. What that leads to is that you don't get the budget, everything falls apart if you don't do it correctly, and so there's a lot at stake."

While the majority of B2B CMOs I interview claim that their marketing activities on average can be linked to between 15 and 30 percent of revenue, Eden sets his sights on 75 percent, and to do that, he explains how one must *automate attentively*:

> If you're building a sales and marketing machine for a company and you want that to generate growth, you want to grow in a smart way. It's about laying foundations. The first foundational block is the systems themselves, and you have to have systems there because you can't just do everything manually; that doesn't really scale. The most common system that people go for first is a CRM system, a Salesforce or Microsoft's CRM, or something along those lines, and usually that ends up being the system of record or where you should go to get the one true version of what's happening. If you are just putting in place a lot of systems and they all have their own reporting, then how do you know which system to believe? You must have a system of record that is one view of the truth.

Allow me to interrupt Eden for a second and put a punctuation point on this last statement. You, the marketer, must have one source of "truth" that the rest of your executive team believes in. This is so important that one CMO I know has created an independent data team that sits between Marketing and Sales, a neutral "Switzerland" of sorts to track and report on all data streams.

Now back to Eden's recommendations: "This CRM system is where opportunities are tracked by the sales team. The sales are recorded as won, and in often cases, that's where the information flows out to billing and contracts, so if you really want to understand what's going on, you have to first architect the CRM system correctly and then you start layering on top of it the other systems, which is often trickier than it appears at first glance."

Eden recommends using Salesforce to come up with what looks like an Excel grid, with three key fields: What's the potential close date? What's the potential sales value? What's the probability of close? For all of their open deals, they click Save once. In terms of time, Eden figured out a way for users to create an "opportunity" in thirty seconds and add more information later.

Eden says, "These things seem like small things, but if you start getting a hundred, two hundred, four hundred, people on Salesforce and you want to get adoption, you have to solve those sorts of things. Part of it could be having offshore people do the data entry and marketing for salespeople so they don't ever type in any information. Part of it is workflow things and making those workflows easier. Part of it is just making it so that when they come in for the day, everything they need to do is organized for them. And if people are out sick, the managers can reassign that work to other people, for example."

Respecting your fellow employees' talents and not forcing them to do stuff they're not good at is smart management. So, we've got Salesforce, and all the data is in there. What's the next tech thing that Eden adds on? Marketing automation. In this area, Eden is perfectly comfortable recommending any of the major players, including Eloqua (Oracle), Marketo (Adobe), and HubSpot. Although these vendors would stridently disagree, in truth, they all work in very similar ways, and the cost is actually comparable. The level of effort to set up, configure, and administer a system is where you'll find the variance.

RAMPING UP YOUR TECH STACK

Another tech-stack wizard I'd like you to meet is Rebecca Stone, currently the CMO at Cisco Meraki. I caught up with Stone in 2019 when she was the VP of marketing at LiveRamp, a data connectivity provider for the marketing community. Five years earlier, Stone had started from scratch, building a demand-generation engine that ultimately accounted for 60 percent of the company's sales pipeline. As you will recall from the previous section, that's at least three times higher than most B2B CMOs.

At the time of our interview, Stone recalled having thirty to forty different technologies in place, segmented primarily among "the core" of Salesforce and Marketo, a "digital tech stack," and a "measurement tech stack." She noted that it was a bit larger than most because the teams of sales development representatives (SDRs) reported to her, and sales support tends to be tech intensive. In recalling the journey to build out their stack, Stone advises, "You have to be extremely focused on process and data, and you have to drive that focus from everybody in the organization. You have to understand how your data is flowing through, where there are gaps, and insist that everybody from the marketing assistant to the top salesperson is following the process to record and keep all of the data."

Staffing, as I mentioned earlier, is also critical. Stone shares, "We have three core marketing-ops team members. I think we could probably use one or two more, but we also have a sales team that sits outside of our team who helps to support some of the sales development components of that tech stack and who manages almost all of Salesforce. And then we have two to three people who are day-to-day users, who are Marketo certified and who are certified in a couple of our other programs."

Stone also suggests patience when you start out, advising: "Do not get too big of an appetite in what you can accomplish, because it is a very, very long journey. Set your sights toward a big thing, a big goal that's a ways away, but figure out the small steps that you can take to get there." And what does "there" look like? Stone shares that her analytics team "built some really, really cool models that predicted the results of marketing dollar investments on both revenue and pipeline."

Stone concludes: "Our lead analyst swore it was ninety-eight percent accurate, and I would have been happy at eighty percent—let's face it, knowing this is the Holy Grail for marketers."

So where does that leave us? When it comes to *automating attentively*, please keep one critical rule in mind: the tech you buy is only as good as the team you have to operate it. If you're a new CMO, make sure you have the best marketing operations manager you can find. Stone notes she's "worked with our head of marketing ops at four different companies, so we know each other, we trust each other, we know what to expect from each other, and he understands where I'm trying to get." In the end, Stone says: "You have to have very strong people in order to run a lean team."

KEY TAKEAWAYS

- Keep your MarTech investment under 10 percent of your total marketing budget.
- Don't add tech without budgeting for the staff time required to leverage it.
- Conduct a MarTech audit at least once a year and weed out the underutilized.

CHAPTER 12

TEST TO TRIUMPH

Summary: Build a culture of experimentation. Reserve 10 percent of your media budget for category-busting tests. Celebrate the failures too.

We've come a long way since *clearing away the clutter* in Chapter 1. Armed with your distinctive purpose-driven story; a pithy yet well-designed marketing campaign that engages employees, cultivates customers, and sells via service; and just the right amount of MarTech, we're now ready to experiment like crazy. Let's do it.

By the way, your CEO will thank you for holding this step until you've laid down the foundation for your brand and related marketing activities. It also makes it a lot easier to experiment once you have a control to test against. It's the essence of the scientific method. Form a hypothesis. Test it. Change a variable. Test again. Or as a legendary yet unknown shampoo bottle copywriter once scribed "rinse and repeat."

There's more to this step than simply testing variables. The bigger idea is to create a culture of experimentation within your department and ideally throughout the organization. This is where a CMO can have an inordinate impact on the culture of a company.

Nathan Rawlins, the CMO of Lucidchart, which produces software for making charts, was approached by an employee with a goofy video that explained a flurry of memes about dogs. The twist was that the video used the company's chart-creation software to tell the story. And importantly, the videos were both funny and topical. Given their "culture of experimentation," Rawlins decided to let the video go up on YouTube and see what happened. A few weeks later, that video had generated millions of views after trending on Reddit. Watchers were suggesting other meme topics, and Rawlins let his team produce a whole series of these. By the end of 2020, these videos had generated more than 120 million views with only a few thousand in media spending. (You can hear Rawlins's inspiring story on our podcast episode "3 Tips for Your Next Viral Marketing Campaign.")

It is worth noting that Rawlins was unable to convince his web team to feature these videos anywhere on the homepage of LucidCharts.com. They warned Rawlins that the website's conversion rates would in all likelihood decline. In sum, they were saying that every inch of the homepage should be devoted to driving sales. Period. No fluff. To me, this continues to be a lost opportunity, not just to connect the dots between a viral sensation and the product but also to inspire customers and employees to have fun with their tool. Without this emotional connection to the brand, Lucidchart is just a functional tool, one that could be replaced without a backward glance.

WHAT TO TEST

In theory, every aspect of your B2B brand strategy and marketing program is testable. In practice, testing everything is likely to drive you and your team bonkers and will not be worth the tremendous energy required nor the delays it can cause. Which means you'll need to focus, using testing as a means of trying new things and driving innovation versus the quixotic pursuit of perfection.

On the definitely-worth-testing list:

- **Media channels:** Just make sure you add one new channel at a time and have a way of measuring results. For example, if you add out-of-home ads like billboards, think about doing so in just a few markets first so you can track your website traffic on a geographic basis.

- **Virtual event experiences:** With physical events off the table in 2020 and most of 2021, many marketers are experimenting with a wide range of virtual events. Depending on the audience and the objective, these range from cooking classes with celebrity chefs to employee-led yoga classes to hiring world-famous speakers for an elite group of CEOs. Variations of these are easy to test and replicate if successful.

- **Event experiences:** Physical events are a great opportunity to test different ways of engaging your targets. Most trade show booths are boring. Try something that is unexpected yet still supports your brand story. Your employees will thank you, and, most likely, your customers and prospects will too.

- **Employee engagement activities:** More and more companies are turning to employees for fresh ideas, ranging from internal process improvements to new product development. Some companies dedicate a day a month to innovation projects. Find a frequency that works for you and let your employees loose on the biggest challenges you're currently facing—they'll appreciate just being asked, and you'll appreciate the ideas they generate. Make sure that at least one of the ideas is pushed forward for further testing.

SHOULD YOU TEST YOUR B2B BRAND PURPOSE?

Since in Chapter 3, we prescribed *pouncing on your purpose*, and given the critical importance of getting your brand purpose right, you'd think we'd also have this on our must-test list. But, surprise, surprise, this is not the case. There are a number of reasons we don't typically test brand purpose. First, the purpose expresses a core belief of the executive team and reflects the foundational aspiration of the organization;

therefore, it is not really a debatable topic. Second, and perhaps more importantly, your B2B brand purpose only becomes real through your actions over time. Your employee activities, your customer experience, and your marketing make your purpose real. Without consistent actions behind the purpose, it's just an empty promise. Sure, you could test a series of statements and get gut reactions to these from your audiences, but these folks would just be reacting to the words. And as we've discussed at length, particularly in Chapters 7 to 9, effective B2B marketing is all about your actions—it's all about doing things.

WHAT HAPPENS IF THE BOARD INSISTS ON POSITIONING RESEARCH?

Go for it. As they say, there's no point in fighting city hall! But the trick is to make sure you are testing your options against the right segment of your audience. When Ben Stuart, CMO of Bank of the West, wanted to make the case for a purpose-driven positioning, he did research among his younger customers who met two key criteria: they were comfortable with technology, and they were influencers whom other people came to for advice. Explains Stuart, "If we could win over younger urban customers who were techno savvy and opinion leaders in their circle, then that would be a great acid test for other concentric circles around that audience." He adds, "We did four different cells of two hundred respondents in four different cities across our footprint, and we ended up testing initially a range of six positions down to three positions, and then there was a clear winner."

BUILDING A CULTURE OF EXPERIMENTATION

A lot of companies celebrate the successes of their employees. Top salespeople are rewarded with lavish prizes. Some companies offer annual awards to outstanding achievers in other areas. But what about the weekly innovations, the little improvements that can snowball into bigger gains? Trish Mueller, the CMO of Home Depot from 2011 to 2016, made employee-driven innovation a top priority. In our interview back in 2016, Mueller noted: "We have built a dynamic culture of curiosity and courage, and we encourage a fast test-and-learn mentality across the entire team. Innovation is definitely a team sport, with ideas coming from team members at any level or rank."

Importantly, Mueller's approach is not just to celebrate the successes, although there was plenty of that. Explains Mueller, "I personally recognize our team accomplishments every Friday in a formal communication that goes out to the entire marketing team. I also recognize team members individually with thank-you notes and shout-outs in our monthly all-hands meetings. Additionally, we awarded a special quarterly innovation award, called the Big Swing award, which recognizes a person or a team for taking a swing at exploring new ideas, which helped us learn—even if the idea may not have worked out as we originally thought. During the all-marketing-team presentation, we lean more on what we learned in the recognition versus whether it failed or succeeded."

ALLOCATE AT LEAST 10 PERCENT OF THE BUDGET TO EXPERIMENTATION

When budgets are tight, experimentation may seem like a luxury, but allow me to share a story that proves the opposite. Caroline Tien-Spalding is the CMO of Aptology, a Silicon Valley–based SaaS start-up that helps companies increase and track the performance of their sales team. Tien-Spalding began as CMO in May 2019 when the economy was booming and leads were flowing in abundance. Nonetheless, she allocated 20 percent of her budget to experimentation, specifically for digital events and to test multitouch email/social campaigns enabled by SalesLoft. As with all other B2B marketers, the pandemic forced Tien-Spalding to cancel the company's physical events in March of 2020, which accounted for 50 percent or more of its budgets and lead flow. But unlike most marketers, she was ready to pivot in a matter of hours, as "the twenty percent experimentation budget suddenly became the eighty percent," making her both prescient and a hero.

Setting aside at least 10 percent of your budget for experimentation is a trademarked move of the renegade marketer. It could save your bacon in an emergency, open up new opportunities when times are good, and reinforce your personal commitment to driving innovation, a signal both your team and your leadership will appreciate.

SETTING UP A SKUNKWORKS

Large companies are notoriously slow at recognizing new market opportunities and even slower at responding to them. Clayton Christensen identifies this challenge in his seminal book, *The Innovator's Dilemma*. If you're a marketer at a big company, your best chance of developing true innovations is to propose a "skunkworks," which can operate like an independent start-up without the constraints of the larger organization. It is in these skunkworks where *testing to triumph* can really prove itself.

One CMO who found success with this approach is Karen Jones of Ryder System. In our 2019 interview, Jones noted that "eighty-five-year-old companies like Ryder have a really hard time innovating and changing their stripes." But given a board-of-directors mandate to think about the future of "the transportation logistics industry," she led a task force to initially identify threats to their current business model and then workshop solutions. Among the four opportunity areas identified, Jones zeroed in on asset sharing. "We call it Airbnb meets Match.com for trucks," explained Jones, who "had the privilege of leading the development of that product, which is even cooler for a CMO." Cool, indeed.

The product, eventually called COOP by Ryder, is an app that enables truck owners to share their trucks. Having discovered that trucks sit idle 24 percent of the time, this app created a marketplace for this "unused inventory." Given organizational fears about this app cannibalizing Ryder's primary business, Jones opted to test the service one market at a time, starting initially with current Ryder customers. "We started the product in Atlanta because there was a huge density of truck volume in that particular market, and we've grown now through the state of Georgia, we took on all of Florida, and this year we're headed to Dallas," she shared.

Note the measured rollout. That's another part of *testing to triumph*. Knowing that customers responded favorably, initially representing

60 to 70 percent of the transactions, Jones turned up the marketing volume with "outdoor billboards, digital advertising, search advertising, all the things that you would expect us to do," shared Jones. This resulted in a shift in the app user base to 70 percent brand-new customers to the company, which had been the goal from the beginning. Jones explained, "It's an amazing mix, and that just gives us the opportunity to continue to upsell other services throughout the Ryder portfolio." She concluded, the app "has absolutely beaten all of our expectations."

ABT: NOT AMERICAN BALLET THEATER—ALWAYS BE TESTING

In Chapter 11, we talked about the importance of *automating attentively* but skimmed over one of the fastest-growing MarTech segments, account-based marketing (ABM). Why? Well, it made better sense to save that for this chapter, since testing is such a critical part of ABM success. To learn more about ABM, in 2018, I caught up with Peter Isaacson, then the CMO of Demandbase. In the CMO role from 2014 to early 2021, Isaacson helped that company create the ABM category and then drive successive years of explosive growth, including the pandemic year of 2020.

According to Isaacson, implementing an account-based marketing strategy is all about identifying the right target accounts. Then, you must uncover the right buying committees and decision-makers within that account. Using specific intent signals can help you accomplish those goals. When done correctly, intent signals allow you and your team to understand which companies are already researching your category and your firm. Intent signals are no longer limited to simply noticing when a company fills out a form on your website but can be identified in a wide variety of behaviors depending on the product. For example, if you suddenly notice ten different people from the same company looking at your website, there is a very good chance they are doing a serious evaluation. Similarly, a visitor that watches your demo video or uses your ROI calculator could very well be signaling they are getting ready to buy.

Account-based marketing is not something that can be ignored in the B2B marketing space. While all marketing is supposed to be highly targeted, ABM enables marketers to track the intent signals of their primary audience while putting highly personalized ads in front of that same target. It's a one-two punch that's putting ABM platforms like Demandbase and 6Sense on most B2B CMOs' shopping lists.

However, Isaacson has found that many people new to ABM strategies make three main mistakes that prevent them from fully succeeding. They are:

1. Not engaging the sales department teams in the new strategy
2. Not aligning with the right target accounts
3. Tackling too many areas of ABM all at once

He proposes that marketers engage with the sales teams from the start to eliminate confusion down the road. He also explains that your former strategies for finding the right target accounts may no longer be effective and that starting small with ABM is the best way to approach the new strategy. To achieve better results, Isaacson advises marketers that are new to ABM to take things slow and steady. Or in other words, *test to triumph*!

Isaacson explains, "It's really about identifying where you are having the biggest challenges with your marketing. First of all, selecting the right accounts is job one, and making sure you're taking a very informed and data-based process in selecting those accounts. Once you do that, most companies we talk to have a big challenge at the top of the funnel. They have identified their right accounts, but they're not making it over to their website, engaging with the content, or taking that first step and doing that investigation on your company. Using advertising to specifically target those accounts is a great first step for most companies because it gets them engaged where you can create a web experience specifically for those companies."

A TRIUMPHANT TEAM

It is worth noting that *testing to triumph* will keep you and your team fresh no matter how long you're on the job. Testing means you can be open to more ideas from more sources inside and outside of your organization. Testing puts the fun back into marketing, fun that can get lost in the pressure to deliver high-quality leads to your sales teams. The cool CATS use testing to build a culture of experimentation, one open to extraordinary possibilities and unbeatable results.

KEY TAKEAWAYS

- Allocate 10 to 20 percent of your marketing budget for experimentation.
- Encourage your team to come up with innovative ideas that you can test.
- Celebrate home runs and strikeouts to cultivate a culture of experimentation.

EPILOGUE

PULLING IT ALL TOGETHER

Alrighty then, we've reached the point where you need to turn the preceding insights into actions. Hopefully you picked up several ideas that you can put into practice right away while you begin the longer journey of courageous strategy development, artful ideation, thoughtful execution, and application of the scientific method. Lest you think I'm throwing you to the wolves, we've assembled a number of additional resources for you on RenegadeMarketing.com, including:

- Strategy worksheet to develop your purpose-driven story statement
- Plan on a Page form
- Resources like the US Trademark review website
- Real-world plans on a page
- Links to all the podcast episodes referenced in the book
- Links to other must-read books

And finally, if you would like to review your purpose-driven story statement and or Plan on a Page with me, you can do so as part of a limited-edition package that includes a personalized version of the hardcover book and a forty-five-minute consultation. Learn more about this option on RenegadeMarketing.com.

Now off you go—go build an unbeatable brand and join the cool CATS as a renegade marketer—and don't forget to let me know how it's going.

ACKNOWLEDGMENTS

The folks that helped me with this book are among the finest CATS I know.

In the Courageous category, I'd start with my wife, Linda Cornelius, who steadfastly supported this endeavor, proofing draft after draft, challenging specious sidetracks and giving up weekend "we time." More significantly, she gave me the courage to keep going, even when the early drafts were not hitting the mark. Then there are the more than four hundred chief marketing officers who shared their stories, warts and all, with me over the last ten years, several of whom you've already met. I take my hat off to their ongoing courage to fight the good fight, to turn marketing into a force of good.

In the Artful arena, I'd first like to thank the Renegade creative combo of Alan Irikura and Anne Rothschild, both of whom help me see more creatively, whose talents have no bounds, and whose work keeps Renegade humming. Then I'd like to thank Sam Beck and Melissa Caffrey, two Renegades who do all the behind-the-scenes production work to make my weekly podcast worth appearing on and listening to, the podcast that is the source of most of the quotes in this book. As copy development editors go, I couldn't have asked for a more artful one than Chris Murray. This book is just plain better, more coherent, and more readable because of his skills. Then there's the team at Girl Friday Productions, who turned the manuscript into the artfully designed book you've just read. Unless you've listened to it, in which case, let's thank the production team at Audivita Studios for their artful voice direction, getting the most out of this amateur narrator's larynx.

In the Thoughtful troop, let's begin with Caroline Tien-Spalding, CMO of Aptology, whose careful reading of the first one hundred pages saved you, dear reader, from all sorts of superfluousness. I'd also like to thank Brent Adamson of Gartner, who shared his insights via four separate podcast interviews, insights that permeate this book. To my eldest brother, Rick, who took the time not just to read this book but also to think through how it might be extended to a course or training program (more on that on RenegadeMarketing.com sometime soon). And to Stephanie Isaacs, the ever-thoughtful client services director at Renegade, who makes sure that everything the creative team and I dream up (that's worth doing) actually happens.

As for the Scientific scholars, I'd first like to thank Kathie Johnson, CMO of Talkdesk. Kathie is the real deal when it comes to measuring marketing, and I'm so grateful for her tutorials, specifically a one-on-one session in 2020 in which she walked me through every single metric calculation. Similarly, I'd like to thank Chandar Pattabhiram, CMO of Coupa, who has helped me understand how to translate marketing metrics into language CEOs and boards of directors will both understand and value. And finally, I'd like to thank both Eric Eden, CMO of Postclick, and Rebecca Stone, CMO of Cisco Meraki, my gracious tutors in all things MarTech.

INDEX

ABOUT THE AUTHOR

Drew Neisser is the founder of Renegade, the award-winning strategic boutique for B2B innovators, and CMO Huddles, the only membership organization exclusively for B2B CMOs. Uniquely wired as both strategist and writer, Drew has helped dozens of CMOs build unbeatable brands and told the stories of over four hundred marketing CATS via his top-rated podcast, Renegade Thinkers Unite, and his column for *Ad Age*. Neisser's first book, *The CMO's Periodic Table: A Renegade's Guide to Marketing*, which published in 2015, features interviews with sixty-four marketing leaders at top brands, including American Express, Dow, IBM, and SAP.

Ranked among the top B2B influencers, Drew has been a featured marketing expert on ABC News, CNBC, CBS Radio, and Tony Robbins's podcast, among many others. Besides *Ad Age*, he's contributed articles to *FastCompany*, *Forbes*, MediaPost, and CMO.com. A frequent keynote speaker and moderator at industry conferences,

Drew is deeply passionate about the role that marketers and marketing can play to make the world a bit better, if not save the planet.

Diapered at Wells Rich Greene, trained at JWT, and retrained at Chiat/Day, Drew founded the agency that became Renegade in 1993, as well as CMO Huddles in 2020. He earned a BA in history from Duke University, lives in Manhattan with his wife Linda, and is the proud parent of two delightful young adults and a French bulldog named Louie. He currently sits on the boards of the Urban Green Council and the Duke Alumni Association. An avid Ben Franklin fan, Drew's favorite aphorism remains, "Well done is better than well said."

Printed in Great Britain
by Amazon

14606454R00108